AMONG SOME THIEVES

Freshwater

Freshwater Press

United States of America

All Scripture references taken from the KJV of the Bible, unless otherwise noted.

Freshwater Press

First printing 2000

Second printing 2022

AMONG SOME THIEVES

ISBN: 978-1-960150-07-3

Paperback Version

Table of Contents

INTRODUCTION 5

THAT DOORMAT 8

WOULD MAKE A NICE WALL HANGING..........................8

TIME THIEVES 16

PRAYER AGAINST TIME THIEVES 29

MONEY THIEVES...31

Moneylending/Borrowing Prayer...................................63

BLESSING THIEVES...66

SAINT THIEVES..73

PRAYER AGAINST SAINT STEALERS...............................81

JOY THIEVES..83

PRAYER FOR JOY...89

KNOCK-KNOCK 90

YOUR IDEA, THE OTHER GUY'S PROMOTION.............100

Inspired Ideas Prayer 104

SO, YOU USED TO OWN SOME *STUFF*? 105

BABYSITTING: 112

LIVE-IN'S & DROP-OFFS..112

BABYSITTING PRAYER 120

WHINING, BEGGING, PLEADING, ...122

GUILT & LYING..122

GUILT & LYING..127

Emotional Blackmail Prayer..130

THE SYMPATHY CHAPTER 131

THE SYMPATHY PRAYER...144

BUT IT'S FAMILY 146

& SUCCESS BREEDS RELATIVES 146

FEAR IS A THIEF 150

FEAR & COURAGE PRAYER...165

HEALTH THIEVES..169

PRAYER AGAINST HEALTH THIEVES..............................181

LIFE THIEVES 183

AMONG SOME THIEVES..187

OUT FROM AMONG SOME THIEVES PRAYER..............196

Books by this author 198

INTRODUCTION

I started this book a long time ago; long before meeting my husband and long before he gave me the moon. Yes, he gave me the moon—the full moon. I never thought for a moment that it wasn't his to give or mine to receive. So, he gave it, and I received it. Preposterous, you might say. No, I believe that there are plenty of moons to go around. Psalm 50 reads that the world is ours and the fulness thereof. There must be enough to share, because God has given us all the sun, the stars, the moon, and the Earth as an inheritance.

It is God's to give, and we are to accept it. We are to be wise stewards over all the works of His hand; and all that we set our hands to do. We don't have to ascend on high to polish the stars to keep them glimmering, but we do have stewardship responsibilities here.

Adam and Eve were placed in the Garden with dominion and authority, as we are in this world, in our *garden*, where God has placed us. We are without excuse; He has also given us power, ability, and Help to handle all things. We are to watch over the things of God, and that includes all the gifts that God entrusts to us.

Why do we need power, ability, and authority in this *garden*? Because weeds have also sprung up due to the sin nature of man. Weeds have sprung up because of man, himself. The weed seeds were placed in the hands of man by the owner of the weeds, the devil. Man has sown and grown a crop of weeds, and as thieves they rob plants of nutrients, block their sunlight, or deny moisture by soaking up the life-giving water that brings abundance and plentiful harvest.

Just as man is the only one who can sow in this garden, he is the one who reaps there. No one else has authority in this place; it was given to man. The Serpent came in with the weed seed, and the man received it. The Bible doesn't read that man was walking through the Garden one day and suddenly came upon some weeds, then ran out screaming, "A weed, A weed!" No, it came through **his** hand. He received it, and then sowed it.

Can he plead ignorance? No. God told him **in advance** not to do it; not to eat of the Tree of the Knowledge of Good and Evil. But hard-headed man, instead of obedience or faith, believes he will only *know* good or evil by **experiencing** it. He wants to live it, taste it, see it, and sense it with his senses and perceptions. And that's why he has gotten and continues to get into so much trouble.

We have a responsibility to prosper on Earth. We should prosper and be in health, even as our soul prospers, (3John2). So, in the midst of weeds, a flower must grow in a garden, in the midst of adversity, we are to thrive. Even in the midst of inconvenient circumstances, we are to give birth; note how Mary, the mother of Jesus, was surrounded by inconveniences. While we thrive and bring forth new life, we are to be wise, discerning, prayerful; even to *try* every *spirit* so that we are not deceived. (1 John 4:1).

Not just among weeds, but *Among Some Thieves*, we find ourselves from time to time. But with the Word, Wisdom, the Grace of God and by Faith, we can do all things and come through victoriously no matter the weave of the fabric of our life.

Holy Spirit, minister now as we travel this path set before us, even ***Among Some Thieves.***

CHAPTER ONE

THAT DOORMAT

WOULD MAKE A NICE WALL HANGING

"But God, I'm a nice person, I don't want to deal with messy situations, sticky circumstances and strange people who don't know how to act right. I just want to go peaceably through my days, go to church, sing in the choir, and praise the LORD. I'm a peaceful person, LORD. Don't you understand? If I just treat people a certain way – like I want to be treated, then they will realize that they need to act nice. It's the Golden Rule, right God? I learned it in kindergarten. Isn't that in the Bible somewhere?

"But if folk start acting funny, I can just go find another church. I've done it before. If people don't want to act right—well, you just can't make people act right. Right? So, I'll just leave them alone and go on about my business."

There are many more who will put up with the above behavior because they think it's godly. There is many a soul who was raised to be a peaceful individual. There is many a soul who believes their purpose in life is to keep peace in their families, workplaces, and even churches. Peace Makers always seek to diminish or avoid conflict. There is many a soul who does not want to trouble the water or add fuel to fire. There is many a soul who does not want to hurt, anger, disappoint, or expose another, even at the expense of *themselves* being hurt, angered, disappointed, or used.

Martyrs

This category of folk, because of their excessive kindness, compassion or over-gentle demeanor are walked on constantly and tricked sometimes while going with the flow, to keep the peace. They try to keep someone else's definition of peace. These are the People Pleasers. These are the ones who become the doormats. These folk give others what *they* want in time, attention, money, services, and so on, but they aren't usually given to people with the same motives.

What is Peace anyway?

- The state of tranquility or quiet.
- Freedom from civil disturbance.
- The absence of war.

- The state of security or order within a community, provided by law or custom.
- Freedom from disquieting or oppressive thoughts or emotions.
- Harmony in personal relations.
- A command or request for silence, or calm.
- A greeting, or farewell.

Jesus spoke of the peacemakers in the Beatitudes, saying they are blessed and called the children of God, (Matt 5:3-11). You may be saying verbally or by your actions, *"I want to be called a child of God, I want to be called a Peacemaker."* That's understandable since God has called us to peace (1 Cor 7:15); and it is a Fruit of the Sprit.

But the fruit of the spirit is Love, Joy, Peace, patience, kindness, goodness, faithfulness, gentleness and self control. Against such things there is no law, (Gal 5:22).

And we should be peaceful individuals "...and with your feet fitted with the readiness that comes from the gospel of Peace," (Eph 6:15).

Peace is a reward. Peace is part of our armor that we wear *among some thieves.*

..."I am the Lord your God, who teaches you what is best for you, who directs you in the way you should go. If only you had paid attention to my commands, your Peace would have been like a river, ..." (Isaiah 48:17-18).

Even in our quest and personal desire for peace, God did not design us to be doormats. After the fall in the Garden in Eden, the wily Serpent was cursed to crawl on his belly, to be beneath and not above, (Deut 28:13)—not us, not mankind. The Serpent is to be below, and that means under **our** feet. We have authority, ability, and power to trample and tread on him, (Psalm 91:13). The Serpent is to be the doormat, **not us**, but that's not the way it's always been viewed in this world.

There are some other souls who are over-aggressive. They pursue personal gain, fame, or wealth at any cost. There are some who would eagerly trample on the things of God, having forgotten and forsaken Him as their Creator, Provider, and Sustainer. There are some who want the people of God to serve them. Many think that Christians are weak slaves, but they are so wrong. When kindness and generosity is given by a Christian, it is given purposefully. While most Christians try to give folk the benefit of the doubt as a course of practice, while being treated kindly, some try to trick or steal from Christians. These are some of the Thieves among whom we find ourselves from time to time.

There are some who believe that *meek* means weak, but the translation of the word, *meek* means, *like God*. Since Jesus is our role model and we are created in His image and likeness, we should be ferocious as lions, mighty and victorious in conflict, through the power of the Holy Spirit, when the situation calls for it. We should be able to use the sword of the Spirit to rightly divide truth from lie.

Blessed are the peacemakers--, but a Peacemaker in the wild, wild west was a revolver. Sometimes real peace, not just perceived peace may cause a little hurt. Feelings may get hurt or egos may be bruised. Emotions, feelings, or offenses may need to be gotten over. Things may need to be worked through. Understanding and growth sometimes must happen before real Peace can be achieved.

The Serpent is to crawl, not you.

If you are being a doormat in your life while trying to make or keep peace, GET UP! Whether in your family, personal relationships or in your workplace, GET UP! Stand up! When God creates something beautiful, it should be displayed, framed, or highlighted, all to His Glory. God made us as Masterpieces (Eph 2:10), not as doormats. He made us wonderful works of art, in His image and likeness. Therefore, we should always be to the praise of His Glory. Lying down and being trampled on is not praiseworthy.

Have you ever walked up to a door and looked down at the welcome mat and thought, Wow, that's pretty? Haven't you ever seen a decorative door mat that should have been a wall-hanging? If you're a people pleaser, God is saying this to you: *"I made you as a masterpiece, why are you lying down and being walked on? Why are you lying down and being victimized or robbed?"*

The Thief cometh not but to steal, kill, and destroy,

(John 10:10)

Being passive or turning the other cheek, *to excess*, and being taken advantage of is not necessarily Christ-like. We all know the Scripture about kindness and heaping coals, but where is the balance between heaping those coals and *correction in love*? God chastises and corrects those whom He loves. God doesn't heap coals upon us with excess kindness.

Owen is 50 years old. As a child and adolescent, he was mean to his saved schoolmates. Now Owen spends most of his time in jail cells, because coals were heaped on his head; his parents and saved friends kept turning the other cheek instead of telling him the truth or correcting him. Excessive kindness is the hallmark of a doormat. We should correct one another in love. We should develop all the Fruit of the Spirit, kindness included, but not to excess or to our own demise, and the demise of others.

Don't be a doormat! The world even says, *Don't take it lying down*. God says we don't have to take it at all; He says He will fight our battles! (1 Sam 8:20). As you see in the above example, when we are doormats, what have we really done for the one who wants to step on us? Made *them* happy, for the time being?

Can we still have peace, **Among Some Thieves**? We are in the world but not of it. So, yes, we can have peace, abiding peace in Him, even while we are in the world. Jesus said,

My Peace I leave with you, not as the world knows,

(John 14:27), *emphasis added.*

To be a Peace Maker, you must *have* Peace. I used to be a people pleaser, a doormat, but now I'm a Peace Maker. People pleasers are miserable, they don't have the peace that Peace Makers have.

When I was a child, and didn't know any better, I sought my parents' and everyone else's approval. That's normal. But as a young adult that behavior should cease. *Be yourself*, is the advice you start to get at that time. That means be comfortable with who you are, and don't be overly concerned about what people think about you. If the people-pleasing cycle continues into adulthood, it is difficult-to-nearly-impossible to break. Thank God that by the power of the Word of God, redemption from the Curse and by the Power of the Holy Spirit, I am no longer a people pleaser. Now, I'm a Peace Maker, and I like being a Peace maker much better. The Peace Maker has power and authority, while the people pleaser is a powerless doormat and won't ever please anyone anyway.

You may be **among some thieves**, but you can negotiate your way through to the Promise as a Peace Maker. The Scripture says, *Blessed are the Peace Makers,* not blessed are the people pleasers.

CHAPTER TWO

TIME THIEVES

Years ago, I took my niece, April, to her first theater movie; *Time Bandits*. Being three, she enjoyed the popcorn, but talked during the entire feature. The film was about some little people who were able to time travel. In all of her talking, almost 20 years ago, I still clearly recall April asking over and over, *"Aunt Marlene, where did the monster go?"*

Monsters are real to some children, almost real to many, and are an everyday thing to others. But the monster that taunts adults daily, is the one that steals, or attempts to steal Time. I don't mean the kind of time theft where days are missing, where today is Wednesday, but when you wake up tomorrow, it's suddenly Saturday. I'm talking about the time-stealing monsters who cause the misuse and mismanagement of Time. I'm speaking of those people who waste **time** *during* those Wednesdays and Saturdays. The time they are really wasting is theirs but sometimes in doing so, they waste yours, too. They include you in elaborate plans to do nothing and keep you from doing the things you want or need to, or enjoy doing. I call them Time Thieves. Some of these Time Thieves ask you to do things with them, then they are late, very late, or never show up. Time is wasted waiting on them or events that you never get to. Sometimes you may start out on the way to an event but make so many stops on the way that you lose track of time or get sidetracked and never get there. Those people.

It's Saturday

You know better. The call comes. It's about noon. There is such a thing as Caller ID but you haven't gotten around to ordering it from the phone company, or wherever you get it yet. And how do you know it won't be too complicated for you to hook it up and use it? After all, the clock on your microwave is still flashing. Even if you had and checked caller ID, it doesn't matter, really because the same people call your house all the time. Saturday, twelve noon--, *it's the in-laws.*

"Hello," (Mother-in-Law), you might as well say, since you know who's calling.

"Oh, Hi," she blurts out, feigning surprise that you're home and answering your own phone. She hasn't heard the sound of your voice in almost two days. *"What are you two lovebird-newlyweds doing?"* she further inquiries.

"Oh, we were just..." you reach for something to tell her that is not a lie, but you don't think or speak quickly enough.

"Well, we're right around the corner. We got up this morning and thought we would take a drive since the weather was so nice." (That's novel, you think since they give the very same explanation of their thought pattern EVERY weekend. *"We'll be right over. We just wanted to check to see if you were home first, you know—"*

"We were just..." You were still looking for that non-lie to tell the in-laws when you hear the clunk sound of the receiver of the payphone as Mother-in-Law hangs up. At least she called this time, instead of just showing up at the door.

Now, **Mrs.** & Mr. Mother-in-Law, (she's the principal in that relationship), have just taken a casual two-hour drive to your house, as they do EVERY weekend since Mr. and Mrs. Newlywed got married eight months ago. They arrive at the door and come in, making themselves at home. Once let in, they will stay through Sunday evening. The in-laws will just sit and sit. They have no concept of what a visit is, or how long it should last. They may treat the newlyweds out to dinner. They are no expense at all, they just invade treasured newlywed privacy, sitting there as part of the décor. Yes, they have other children, but none so interesting as Mr. and Mrs. Newlywed. And here they are again for the entire weekend—the same weekend that you've been working toward and waiting for all week, so you can do something special with your spouse, your own family, or friends.

"Well," Mrs. Mother-in-Law wants to know, *"Do you have any plans to have children yet? I sure would like some grandchildren. I was going to get you a card for Mother's Day, but then I remembered that you're not a mother—"*

Ooh, that cut, but you've learned not to answer any of the female elder's questions or comments, for fear of losing your temper.

"Oh, I know about my son, but Daughter-in-Law, is that the real color of your hair?"

No response. Is she *still* talking? you think to yourself.

"It doesn't look like you're much of a housekeeper."

"I'm going to take a nap, I have a headache," you interject.

While walking away you hear, *"Daughter-in-law, aren't you going to cook dinner. Can you cook? I've invited some other relatives who live nearby, for supper. You can cook, can't you?"*

"You did what!" you shout, nearly losing your cool.

"You know Cousin Jim and Marcy and their three little ones. They are so cute – anyway, oh I almost forgot, Marcy's mother and sister are in from out of town, so that will be seven, plus us for dinner. Nine. They live in Boston, don't they, Son?"

I did not hear that, you think to yourself, I know I didn't hear that. This is a dream, I'm sleepwalking. I need to finish my nap and wake up. Then you admit, no—it's real. Just like last week.

You've tried many things to bring the weekend torments to your husband's attention, but he doesn't hear or see it. You've tried to shorten or stop the in-law visits but to no avail. You disconnected the doorbell a few weeks ago but heard your husband outside at the crack of dawn checking it the following Saturday, and he usually doesn't get out of bed until 10 am on Saturdays. You've tried unplugging the house phone, but your husband bought new telephone wires to connect to the phone jacks and he wiggles them every Saturday morning, too. He hasn't said anything to you about these "incidents", but you sense he's not far behind your undercover moves, closely checking wires, ringers, bells, and things.

And you're at your wits end, having tried everything from feigning sleep, being in the shower to soaking, more like sulking in the bathtub, but they come anyway. One Saturday you convinced your husband to take you for waffles at 11:00 am, when you got back at 1:00 pm the in laws were sitting in their Oldsmobile in your driveway.

"Oh, we've only been here an hour or so. We don't mind waiting, we knew you'd come back sooner or later," she explains with a happy chuckle.

After that incident, you haven't been able to get him to take you to Saturday brunch again--, at least not *before* they get there.

It's understandable that your husband wants to see his parents; and sometimes you'd like to see yours. Some weekends you'd like to just sit around in a big, sloppy T-shirt, relax in your own home, or go biking with your husband. A round of golf would e nice. Something. Anything. And you've told your husband, more than once, that you'd like to do more things personally, and *as a couple* with him, but he doesn't seem to have heard.

He also hasn't even heard how rude his mother is to you, either. She's good at making comments that he <u>never</u> hears. He's never heard anything ugly she's ever said to you, even when everyone is in the same room. When you finally get the courage to tell him about his mother, he looks at you with that age-old question: *What is wrong with women? Why can't they get along?* Maybe he, along with this father, have tuned out the mean, old matriarch. But you haven't advanced to select deafness yet, as many men have.

If you felt a little love or at least a relationship growing between you and the in-laws, you'd try harder, but it's not getting better, it's getting worse. It's great for your husband when they visit and it's horrible for you. And it's <u>*every*</u> weekend.

Unlike the rest of your co-workers, you've begun to dread Fridays and they are also wondering what's wrong with you.

How can you get the Drop-in-Laws to stop using up your weekend time? You can't at least not by yourself. They obviously aren't there to enjoy your company anyway. If they were. They treat you better. If you chose to do something on your own every Saturday, they'd still come to see their son. Is that a good thing to do for your marriage? Especially being newlyweds? No.

Don't attack your spouse with this book. It is not a weapon against humans. Let it be an instrument of peace. He can handle things with his parents or the two of you can do it together.

What are the possible problems? Once you've ruled out that you're not a snob, you can look at these other possibilities. You're not a snob, are you?

- Spouse hasn't cleaved.
- Mother-in-law and spouse haven't severed the umbilical cord.
- Father-in-law either hasn't assumed or has relinquished his patriarchal authority in the family. Mother-in-law is now wearing the pants.
- Spouse hasn't moved from the child role into adulthood and independence, even in the preceding example, Mr. Newlywed had been living on his own many years prior to the marriage.

Therefore, shall a man leave his father and mother, and shall cleave unto his wife, and they shall be one flesh, (Genesis 22:4).

- His parents don't have a life.

- His parents don't have a relationship with one another.
- His parents don't have a relationship with God, else they'd be at their home church on Sundays. Also, they would know that the Proverbs say, *Don't overstay your welcome.*

Withdraw by foot from my neighbor's house, lest he be wary of thee and so hate thee (Proverbs 25:17).

All of these things use up or waste time, not walking in your position or your purpose wastes time. Hanging out with the non-positioned and the non-purposed wastes your time, unless you've been sent by God to minister to them.

But if the in-laws are sporting the college tuition, mortgage note, car payment, or other expense, you won't or can't get rid of them, unless you're ready to declare financial independence. If you wait until graduation to finally tell them that they come over too often or visit too long, there will be much trauma because they will feel hurt and used.

This is why it is best to wait for independence before marriage. Wait for your position and purpose. Leaving the birth home and the child- parent relationship directly into marriage may not work for all. Families stayed together in the same house in generations past, even after marriage. But not so much, now. Note that it didn't always work well in the old days. Look at the trouble Jacob had with his in-laws, (Genesis 29-31).

A thief, a would-be thief is a master time waster. They sometimes very patiently set up their game. Laban was one such master time waster. He caused Jacob to spend 14 years trying to win Rebecca. If someone habitually tries to waste your time, ask the question, *What do they **really** want from you? What do they want that they are not saying, have not expressed, cannot express or are not planning to express?* Then maybe you can get to the bottom of things and stop wasting time.

Back to the newlyweds. Where are *her* parents all these weekends? If both sets of parents converged on the home every Saturday, what will happen? Probably a disaster. When Margie's mother-in-law asked that they build her a room in their new house, Margie wised up and told her husband she'd agree to it if they could put twin beds in the room and whenever *his* mother visited, **her** mother could visit at the same time and then see how long both mother in-laws could last together. The conversation was never broached again, and the room was never built.

The Wilderness Romance

In-laws and relatives are not the only Time Thieves. What about those girlfriends who call you up to meet for lunch to talk about that single man in their life? When they ask you over and over what they should do, yet they profess to know everything you tell them.

"Is he a Christian--is he saved?" you ask.

"No, not exactly."

Jesus doesn't partially or *inexactly* save people you think to yourself. *"Leave him alone, witness to him, invite him to church; just be a friend,"* you say out loud. You take another bite of your sandwich, thankful that the bread is not as stale as this been-over-it-before subject.

"He's really nice."

"But is he saved," you stress.

"No."

"Then just be a friend."

"Yeah," but he wants more.

"So does the devil."

"I know," she replies, sounding irritated. She hesitates, but says it anyway, "But he is so cute." You knew that was coming.

"And the devil can appear as an Angel of light," you reply dryly with a mouthful.

"I know," she concedes.

And you know that she knows, and *why*? Because she's talked to so many other people about this man. Your girlfriend is searching for someone, *anyone* who will agree with her. Why she is going on about this man when the search should be on, not for a new boyfriend, but the search should be ongoing in her heart as to what is wrong with her. Why does she keep going in circles about this man? She is going around and around as if this man is a Promised Land or something. A promised man?

The Wilderness Romance is another time thief. If he is the man God has for you, here are some characteristics which you might take as signs. Else you might wonder and wander forever.

- You don't have to *fix* the man that God has for you. The one God has for you is already fixed because he is Christ-like or trying to approach perfection. God would not send you an alcoholic or drug addict. Is that what you prayed for? Of course not.

- He is fixed *spiritually*. He is, saved, at least, and Spirit-filled, hopefully.
- He's mentally and emotionally stable.
- He's financially stable and secure. He doesn't make comments about your success or how much money you make or don't make.
- You are compatible with him spiritually. God does not like unequal yokes.
- You two are equal, or at least compatible intellectually, emotionally, and physically.
- You find him attractive physically.
- He finds you physically attractive. You don't have to *win* his attention daily because you are not his **type**, but lucked out and *got him*.

Using common sense, and rejecting amnesia, recall what you prayed for and see if he fits. If you're not sure, ask God as John did: "Is this the one, or do I look for another?" Then wait for the answer. You did pray about your spouse-to-be, didn't you?

God has not promised you a man that you have to give birth to, diaper, dress, or take care of until he finds a job. God has not sent you to correct his substance abuse problem or pay his bills. He has not sent you a man that you have to love **more** than his mother, his ex-wife or any previous girlfriend so he can stop abusing women verbally, emotionally, or even physically. God did not send you a man to drive your car for you because his vehicle is not, how shall I say it, in existence yet--, it hasn't manifested, yet.

PRAYER AGAINST TIME THIEVES

Heavenly Father, most wonderful and merciful God, in the Name of Jesus, I repent of having wasted time in coming to accept Jesus as my Lord and Savior. I repent of having wasted time in disobedience, rebellion, or procrastination. I come to You knowing that You have created all good things in Heaven and Earth and given them to us. One such gift is Jesus Christ. Thank You, Father.

In your Word, You have authority over time. You, Lord, are able to make the sun and the moon stand still. You are Sovereign Lord. You can restore stolen and lost Time.

In the Name of Jesus, I stand against situations and people who waste the precious Time you've given me. I stand against the people who may be lost or wandering, who inadvertently or purposefully waste my Time. Lord, as those people come to me in the Name of Jesus, give me a word in season for them. Help me to point them to You either by word, deed, or testimony. Then give me strength and boldness, Lord, to speak when I should speak and Wisdom to know when it's time to refrain from visiting and part company.

You, Lord, can deliver me from time wasters so I can use my time wisely to bless self, home, family, and others all to Your glory. Help me to see what I should see in people so I can know if to spend time with them or move on.

Forgive me for wasting anyone's time, -- boyfriend, girlfriend, husband, wife, Ex, --anyone's time in the Name of Jesus.

I repent today, and purpose to be a wise steward over my time and not to hinder anyone else's or use up their precious God-given time. Thank you for the victory. Amen.

CHAPTER THREE

MONEY THIEVES

--If you don't choose a charity, one will be chosen for you.

This chapter is not about burglars, robbers, pickpockets, scam artists, convicted criminals or muggers. It is about saved folk.

I once lent everyone I knew, who was prone to borrow money from me, fifty dollars so they could all owe me money and not be in a position to ask for more. Owing money, they would keep their distance, as is human nature. The plan worked pretty well except for one wise guy who paid me back promptly, and then borrowed a hundred dollars, which I haven't seen since.

It takes all kinds to make a world. Those who never have any money are that *kind*. We are talking about adults here, not preschoolers. The ones who forget their checkbook everywhere they go, except the places that don't take checks, then they have their wallets or their stash of cash that they've put in

Compartment Four of the filing cabinet they are toting around calling a handbag and wondering why their shoulder and back hurt. Those people.

Does it sound like I'm talking about women here? I am. I'm also talking about men. But women have some issues about money that I am sharing from a firsthand view. As a waitress, through college, all waitstaff in more than one restaurant where I worked, would try to avoid a group of women patrons. Have you ever noticed? It's not because you're Black, White, purple, green, tall, well-dressed, good-looking, or different. It's not just because you're female. ***It's because you are female, and in a group of females.***

I'll tell you why: Women diners have a bad reputation. Women diners are hard to satisfy; you can't serve them fast enough, the food doesn't taste right, as if grandma is in the kitchen, their own personal recipe for hot wings is better, or they could make it better than that at home. *Then stay there!* They eat half of it, send the rest of it back and want it taken off their check. And, to top it all off, they do not want to pay at the end of the meal. Not to mention, the often-non-existent tip.

In groups like that, often when the check finally gets paid, it's by the woman who's stuck at the table after the race has begun to *leave first*. I know because I've been the woman left at the table on numerous occasions. Pagers go off, cell phones ring, pantyhose run, irons left on at home are suddenly remembered and children have to be picked up **immediately**. Did I mention that I've been the last one left at the table many times?

One day I was invited to lunch by Karen, and two other church members, Angel, and Theresa. I thought we were meeting to discuss intercessory prayer at the church, but I soon found out it was Angel's birthday. It was a planned birthday luncheon for Angel, at her favorite spot, Red Lobster. *That's nice*. I didn't know whether or not to feel honored.

At the end of the meal, Karen decided that since it was Angel's birthday, Angel didn't have to pay. Then Karen decided that since Theresa was divorced, with two small children, that she didn't have to help pay for Angel's birthday lunch, either. Which left her and me. I was a new member of the church (four months) and wanted to make friends. As not to rock the boat, I paid for my meal and half the cost of Angel's birthday meal. Trusting God, and having faith that when my birthday came around -- , well this must be how they do it at this church.

As a note, when my birthday came around, nothing happened. I received a birthday card from the church office approximately one month after my birth date. Friendship never progressed with Angel. Theresa moved out of the state, and Karen and I became loosely acquainted. End of the people portion of that story. We never did discuss intercessory prayer, either. But I still trust God. If He hasn't returned that act of giving back to me yet; He will. If He has, I praise Him; and I trust He will bring it to my remembrance. I trust God.

But there is more to the reputation that women have earned. When four men eat out and the bill is $80, for example, they all put down $20 plus something for a tip. Not women. They practically shred the check with comments such as *"I only had water, and the iced teas were 95 cents."*

Or *"The dessert you had was fifty-cents more than the one I had."*

After their meals are ingested these women who just dined together become strangers. When the check comes, they become as enemies.

"Miss, can you bring us separate checks?" The same waitress, who asked with a smile, at the beginning of this meal, now turned into an ordeal, if one check would do, and everyone had agreed, is now

still waiting on all of you. Table 30 has been seated, and they are looking for some iced tea, water, anything; they are parched. An order for Table 34 is in the kitchen under the lights, dying as they say; I'll say getting mushy.

While at Table 32, your table, you all are quibbling overpaying what will amount an expenditure or savings of one or two dollars. These same quibblers do not consider the sales tax, which on food is higher than non-food tax in many cities.

So, the server is stiffed (not tipped) by your table, or you leave her the change, which will amount to 5 percent, if even that. Table 34 is irritated; her tip is diminished there. The people at Table 30 are starving, her tip is diminished there before she even has had a chance to meet them. Or, if she uses Wisdom and goes to those other tables while you all nitpick, you will feel justified in leaving her **no tip at all**. But your indecision and unwillingness to cooperate with the people you came with should not affect the waitress's tip.

(At the time this book was written), a waitress was paid about $2.75 per hour; she depends on tips and gratuities to earn a living. She works with the expectancy, and need, of a certain salary. Don't you? Refereeing the table when the check comes is not part of waitressing duties. Who comes into your workplace looking like a business prospect, but ends up *decreasing* your productivity and earning potential? This is what has happened in the previous example.

If I've told you something that you don't know, then bless God. If this doesn't apply to you, then thank God.

I have never in my history of waiting tables seen a man come back to a table and **remove a tip** after his wife has left it there. Women, I cannot say the same of you. I have personally seen women come back to a table, or just turn around as her husband (date) walks ahead, and **take the dollar**, the *whole* dollar, that the man left for the server.

When that tip left the hand of the tipper, it became the waitress's or the waiter's money. If anyone else picks up that money, it's called stealing. Didn't your momma, Sunday school teacher, or pastor teach you that's stealing? Yet, we complain that we are **among some thieves**. If God called a meeting in the Ladies Room, would there be a Tip Money Thief looking at you in the mirror? Would there be tip money in your hand?

I'm talking about more than waitresses and tips. I'm talking about attitudes about money, cooperation, honor, and respect for one another. Yes, it's important to care about the people in your party and your friends whom you know. And it's important that you pay your portion of the check willingly. What about the waitress, whom you don't know? Must she take less because you don't know her, or because you don't think you'll see her again? If she were your own child, would she still be a *nobody*? What if she were your pastor's daughter, would she still be nobody? What if she were coming to join your church tomorrow and give her testimony, which included you! Her testimony might be how the Lord delivered her from a table of cheapskate women, who sent her home with no money and a headache.

You need a Waitress, but she needs a WITNESS! By the way, who at your table can **witness** to a waitress if she's unsaved, if all of you Christian ladies are acting like that? I really didn't want to say this, but especially on the list of people waiters try to avoid are cheapskate women, in large groups, is professed Christians. Too many, for some reason, have decided that they want to test the *favor of God* in restaurants, and try constantly, consistently, and continually to get free food. People, even if buffalo wings were modern-day manna, ask God for free food, don't try to trick waitresses and restaurants.

I've personally heard groups of waiters standing just watching a person eat, saying, *"The Christian is here."* They all expect that the *"Christian"* will find something to complain about so they will get a discount on their meal, or not have to pay at all. I've personally seen it happen many times in my college history of waiting tables. And it's not always the same "Christian." The staff cringes when a group of *Christians* come in, especially if all female.

That doesn't mean get an attitude, or don't go out to eat. It means start to be cognizant of how you:

- Represent God, yourself, and the Body of Christ in restaurants, or wherever you are.
- Treat people who serve you.

Of note, **waiters** treat each other exceptionally well, especially when visiting each other's restaurants. They honor one another. As **servants**, we should be able to recognize and appreciate another **servant**, *Saved or Unsaved*, and treat them very well. Remember the childhood ditty, it takes one to know one?? If you truly are a **servant** (of the Most High God), you should be well able to recognize one. **Jesus was a servant**. What if Jesus waited your table at the Red Lobster? How would you tip Him?

I describe this restaurant server as a female because women don't treat male servers as badly as they treat other women. Perhaps I should ask, what if Mary, the mother of Jesus was your server --, how would you treat and tip her?

Honor the check when the waiter brings it.

Honor and respect those who serve you.

As servants, we should be able to

Recognize and appreciate

Another servant and treat them

Very well.

Time Is Money

But I'm also building on the first chapter, *Time Thieves*. If you have not treated the waitress right, tipped her reasonably or generously, then you have stolen Time from her. If you picked up the tip money, any of it, then you also stole money from her. What if your boss waited until the end of the week then critiqued you before deciding *if* you'd get paid, and what you'd get? Every week?

What if your boss laid your money on the table, then before you picked it up—he took it back? What if you were completely at his mercy? The waitress is at your mercy and subject to your honor.

Does that make you feel powerful, or benevolent? We are at God's Mercy, does He treat us with Justice, or with Mercy and Grace, most often? Mercy and Grace.

Can God trust you to do what's right? Learn how He responds, then you'll know what to do. And since we want all want grace, favor, and mercy, we should give it. You are presented with excellent opportunities every day to practice your Christianity and the principles of God. It's what you do with these opportunities that give you promotion or earn punishment from God.

Maybe you just can't bear the thought that the waitress will get the *whole* $5 that's left on the table. She won't, the waitress has, to **tip out**. That means she has to tip the busboy, the bartender, even if you don't drink alcoholic beverages. In some cases, the cook gets part of her tips for the evening. If she doesn't tip them well, they may think she's holding back on them, and she'll get poor service from them on her next shift. If she doesn't earn enough to tip them well and still take something home, she'll probably quit her job.

Do you need to know all of this to do what's right?

Where did God go in all this? He's right here. Just like the waitress uses some of the money she's received to tip out, we are to bring our tithe into the storehouse, **so there maybe meat in my house,** (Malachi 3:10).

Maybe you just can't bear to think the preacher will get that *whole* $50 that you put in the offering plate. He won't. The tithes and the offerings are to the Lord and the House of God. It takes money to run a house. You have one, don't you? You know how much is involved in keeping your household going, whether you have kids or not. Electricity, telephone, internet, mortgage, and insurance are a few household concerns that require funds. Look at all God is doing. It takes money to run a planet and a universe. God uses that money to bless you and others in the Kingdom.

God has all of His promises recorded in the Book. He doesn't change; God is not fickle.

Ignorance

Maybe people don't tip or tip appropriately because they don't know fractions. Gordon was pleased that he skipped 7th grade Math and that "the system" never caught, that he missed it. He felt that he really *got over*. Unfortunately, it's the class where they taught fractions. Gordon, to this day doesn't know what a fraction or percentage is, or how to figure it. Since he can't figure fractions, then how is he tithing?

You also need to know fractions and percentages to figure out a multitude of daily things from grocery store purchases to restaurant service tips. The old movie scenes where a big shot said to the cute little waitress, *"Keep the change, honey,"* is not our model. That may have been substantial money in the 1940's or 50's, but $0.37 tip on a meal that costs $21 is an insult to the server.

If you don't know fractions or how to figure them, get some teaching. Take a class or get a book on it. Maybe your child can help you. Bless your child by teaching them tithing at an early age. Take the time to at least figure out what your tithe is on your regular paycheck, so you'll be accurate to the Lord.

Consecrated Money

We are to bring our money into the House to sanctify the money.

> ..I will consecrate their gain unto the Lord and their substance into the Lord. Of the whole earth, (Micah 4:13b).

We are to bring our gifts to God, into the House of the Lord, and consecrate them unto the Lord of the whole Earth.

Money put in our hands can be used for worthless endeavors or sown to create valuable plantings. If the money is of the world, it is used for worldly things, it will bring forth weeds. If it is consecrated, sanctified, blessed, and set apart by us, by bringing it into the House of God, He can use it to prosper us and His Kingdom.

A gallon jar half filled with water can bless half the number of thirsty people as one that is completely filled. Or, it can bless the same number of people half the way. The money, gifts and tithes we bring into the House of God is sanctified, consecrated, and accursed for the use of God. **Accursed** means set aside for God's use. If it is misused, then it will curse the person misusing it. It's all built in to the laws already established by God, So you don't have to look to see what the preacher's car or house or his wife's hat and pumps look like. God does that and He's looking at your hat and shoes also. As well, God is looking at what you put in the tithe and offering baskets.

When you bring your money in for consecration think of it as *spiritual money laundering*. Even gangsters know to launder money. When criminals do it, it's so the money will appear as good, clean money. But when God sanitizes your money, it **becomes** good and clean for good and clean use. You take money gotten out of the world--, workplace or wherever, and you consecrate it to God, placing it into God system. The next week, if you want or need God to bless you, He's got something with which to work. God doesn't want you to have to go around impoverished and needing to borrow money. I'm not saying that there is a shortage of money to God, but the consecrated money. Where is it? God is depending on us to consecrate it unto Him.

Consecrating this money doesn't just bless you, it is for ministry to build the Kingdom of God and bless those less fortunate than ourselves. Blessed money blesses people.

Ten Percent

What you yield to God He can use, (2 Timothy 2:22). If God is using it, then He's making something awesome out of it. He made the heavens and the earth out of darkness and void, (Genesis 1). He made man out of clay. In the following He made miracles out of the small portion they gave. The widow's mite, (Mark 12:42). The little woman of Arafat, (1 Kings 1:7). The widow with the two sons and the cruse of oil, (2 Kings 4:1-8).

God asks for 10%. What can God make out of 10 percent? ONE HUNDRED PERCENT. only God can do that.

What can you do with 10% tithe? God is the only one who can use 10% and make it into something. Ten percent of the oil needed in your truck will do no good. Ten percent of cake ingredients will not make a cake. Ten percent of your mortgage payment will not even be accepted. Paying 10% of your utility bill will get you a candlelight supper or quiet meditation time as you sit in the dark waiting for the electricity to be turned back on.

The Borrowers

Remember, it takes all kinds. I take issue with the film, *The Borrowers*, which is based on the children's book of the same name. The movie teaches children that stealing is borrowing. In the movie, little people live in a house with humans. They take things to make their homes. They *borrow* things from unsuspecting regular-sized people. Things that turn up missing in your everyday life, that you just can't find, are shown in the Borrower's little house, which is somewhere behind a wall or under a floorboard. The viewing audience sees this, but the movie humans are still in the dark. The scissors you know you left in the top drawer, but just can't find, the Borrowers have them. It's supposed to be cute, but nothing is ever returned--, certainly not ice cream and other things to eat. How do you borrow food if you *eat* it? So, if it's not returned then it's not borrowed; it' stolen.

The movie doesn't show the true consequences of these actions, and may spark the over-active imaginations of children, who may take things that they shouldn't from their own homes, the homes of neighbors and relatives, or even from school. When caught they'll respond that they only *borrowed* them. I'm not movie-bashing; there are some people who want their children to learn these behaviors, but a Christian should not.

To view any movie may be acceptable but it is the parents' responsibility to teach their children and correct wrong teaching. The Bible says in Deuteronomy that we should teach our children at all times. So, if you choose that your child is entertained by this sort of movie, teach him/her the right way. Explain that it is make-believe, it's only a movie.

> And thou shalt teach them diligently unto thy children, and shalt talk of them when thou sittest in thine house, and when thou walkest by the way and when thou liest down, and when thou riseth up, (Deuteronomy 6:7).

This all leads up to those people who **borrow money** just because they can. It's a power surge to them, similar to the gambler's rush of winning cash. They don't *need* the money, they just *like* borrowing it—they prefer using yours instead of theirs. Have you experienced any borrowers who don't return things? Once an acquaintance asked to borrow some money. I said, *"No, because I only have $10. in cash, and I need it."*

He insisted. I again insisted, louder, *"No."*

After a ridiculous conversation, he pulled out a wad of several hundred dollars, laughing and saying, *"I don't need your money, I just wanted to see if I could get it. And I was never going to pay you back either."* (There is something so demonic about that.)

Then there are those people who need to borrow money for a good cause. Which is usually 'cause they want it. And I'm sure you've encountered those people who say they are borrowing money to "help someone else."

Choose a Charity

> *--If you don't choose a charity, one will be chosen for you.*

I had a dream one night in which one of the people that I had lent $50. to at the beginning of this chapter was coming out of a building as I was going in. I was happy to see him, because even in the dream, I remembered that he owed me $50; and fortunately, he had the money in his hand. As I approached him, he turned and handed the money to a person that I knew but didn't particularly care for. He either gave or lent the money to her. I became acutely aware at that moment that I don't know what people are doing with money that I lend them. I don't know to whom they are lending or giving it, and if the money is never paid back to me, then it's a gift to them or to whomever they give it. My charities were being chosen by borrowers. Either directly or indirectly, borrowers who don't repay loans could be choosing your *charities* for you, too.

Borrowing

Speaking of borrowing, have you ever wondered why many professed Christians just can't seem to borrow from banks like other people? Maybe God wants you to trust Him instead of the credit card company or bank. Why would there be a need to believe God for provision when you have provision? When you say things like you want to know Him and His suffering, brace yourself. You're asking for tests. Do you love anyone enough to ask for tests that you might not otherwise get? Because you love your husband or wife, do you want to go through what *they* go through or have gone through, even if it's negative, just so you can **know** them better? Or can they just *tell* you about it?

Well, Jesus could just *tell* me about it.

That's why there's a Bible; God can just *tell* me about a lot of things that are in the Scriptures. Obedience is better than to sacrifice. Instruction and understanding is better than living in hell or going through hell. The Holy Spirit can lead me into all truths. I don't have to experience *everything* firsthand. That was Adam and Eve's mistake with the tree in the first Garden. But when it comes to borrowing, Jesus was never turned down by a banking institution, so that's not part of the **suffering**.

Suffering because of poverty, or having-not is not my idea of being *spiritually evolved*. Jesus was not impoverished either, so that was not part of the *suffering*. Poverty is spiritual because money is spiritual. But poverty is not God's plan for us. Plus, Jesus didn't want for anything, and was not poor, and we are to be conformed to His image. But If God is allowing Christians to not have credit or borrowing potential, there must be a reason for it. (Make sure your profession of Christ is real; don't blame God if you're not walking upright before Him.)

- Maybe He's keeping you out of debt.

- Maybe He's keeping you free or mobile, for evangelism or another ministry.
- Perhaps He's perfecting something in you.

Whatever the reasons, they are bound to be for your good. His thoughts are higher than ours, and His ways are not our ways. But it would be far better to be spiritually mature enough to be *trusted* with good credit. A good name is rather to be chosen than great riches, (Proverbs 2:1). To be trusted to have the ability to shop and make purchases without the fear of going overboard, then having to call on God to bail you out, is better than not having a good name or reputation.

> For the heavens are higher than the earth, so are my ways higher than your ways and my thoughts than your thoughts, (Isaiah 55:9).

Lent Money

You may lend money to a friend, but what will they do with it? To whom are they lending or giving money? You don't know. By lending, have you supported a ministry that you may not approve of? Was it your intention to help someone, possibly unsaved, accomplish their unsaved goals? Whether you answered probably not, or definitely not, the answer is still--NOT. If you *gave* the money away, it's no longer yours and you are no longer **attached** to it.

But if you *lent* it with the expectation of getting it back, you may be thinking or saying, *"I want my money, my money, my money back."* **You are still <u>attached</u> to it and will reap what that money reaps based on where it is used.**

If the person to whom you let the money went into a topless bar where they are practicing *whoredoms* and sorcery (alcohol or drugs), you just contributed to that "ministry." And you just contributed to the enabling of the person to whom you lent the money. You've also just supported the local saloon, making them profits so they can stay in business and corrupt some more people. As with any business, bars, saloons, casinos, and topless dance halls stay in business because they make lots of money and people keep going to them. Now, there you are, a God-fearing church goer, who would never step foot into a place like that, but you just unwittingly *contributed* to the Kingdom of hell.

As steward over your money, you are responsible for where it goes and what it accomplishes.

If you are blessed to be a Christian lender, you have the responsibility to ask what the borrower is doing with *your* money. Banks do it every day of the week, and you also have the right to ask the borrower what they are going to do with the money. Banks don't make a moral judgment when they lend the money, but they do care if the money will be used wisely. If you tell the bank you are going to gamble the $50,000 you just borrowed, the bank may rescind the loan. That's an unsaved banker at an unsaved bank. How much wiser and spiritually astute should you be when you lend money?

Because of stewardship. Money is spiritual, and you have a *spiritual attachment* to your money. If that lent money blesses people, you share in the blessing. If it is used for sin, you will get to share in the iniquity.

Add these types to Money Thieves:

- Folks who say they're *borrowing* when they have no intention of paying you back.
- Folk who lie about what they're going to do with the money you've lent them.

Being under the bondage of sin is no excuse for being a Money Thief. If you can't trust yourself with money, ask for help. You may find that you're not able to handle a lot of other things, if you can't handle money.

Where there is sin, there is a consequence of sin. What is the punishment for lending or enabling someone with gambling, alcohol, drugs, or other sin? I don't know, but there will be one. The wages of sin is death, (Romans 6:23) -- maybe no one will drop dead, but the death of something will ensue sooner or later. I've found with God, the closer your relationship is with Him, the sooner the death or demise of that *something* will be. He chastises those whom He loves. The punishment will come, unless you quickly repent.

On occasion, I would lend money to a friend who was very diligent about paying it back. It started out as small sums of money and eventually it became thousands of dollars at a time. The problem was that every time I lent this friend money, my own bank accounts would be affected adversely. I'd make a math error or some other mistake, such as forgetting to go to the bank to make deposits by bank closing time. I used to think it was me, but oftentimes my cash flow would become very sluggish or dry up completely until he paid me back. I'd be so happy to have the money back because immediately my cash flow would resume or even *increase* when I got my money back. The same money that I would be glad to do without for weeks at a time, I thought, until he borrowed it. Many times, my banker showed me favor and would call me so I could avoid fees and financial set back, but it was still embarrassing and inconvenient.

I started to notice the cash flow problem after the second or third time I lent him money. After asking some questions, I discovered what he was doing with the money I lent him: gambling. Gambling most often includes drinking, witchcraft, and sorcery respectively, so I started reaping negatively, when my *lent* money started going into negative places.

The Solution:

- Ask borrowers what they're going to do with the money you lend them.
- Lend only to those you trust to do what they say they're going to do with the money.
- Count lent money as dead, if possible. (Invested money is not lent money.)

I Would Not Have You Ignorant

I stopped the lending immediately and repented to the Lord for my ignorance. Having refrained from that behavior, I have had no adverse flow in my finances since that time.

Even in the world, ignorance is no excuse for breaking civil law, and ignorance cannot be a defense for breaking spiritual laws, especially since God has it all written down for us anyway. He says through Paul, *I would not have you ignorant*, which may mean I don't want you to be ignorant, so I'm going to educate you. But it may mean, *I would not have you if you were ignorant,* which is a rejection saying, *Go away, I don't want you.*

Have you ever been turned down for a job because of lack of education, either not enough or the right kind? That's because the employer **didn't want you ignorant.** When the opportunity to become un-ignorant presents, take it, take the opportunity to be taught.

Compare the Following Two Classified Ads:

1. Employee wanted. Neither experience, knowledge, nor intelligence necessary. Will train.

2. Employee wanted. College degree a must, 2+ years' experience.

See how they compare? Most people don't know what to do with an ignorant person, and they don't want them. I've never seen the words, "Ignorance a plus," in a classified ad.

Does God know what to do with the ignorant? Yes, Jesus (Rabboni) is a Master Teacher. A teacher is the *only* person who will take the ignorant and care enough or have the ability and the patience to educate them. Thank God. as you come into the Kingdom, you don't have to feel inferior or inadequate. about anything that you don't know about God, the Word or even church. God will take care of you if you apply yourself and try. Be diligent to study, read, listen to sermons, messages, and teachings. We are to *study to show ourselves approved*, (2 Timothy 2:15). God will forgive ignorance of the Word concerning anything, including money, if we repent, study, and apply ourselves to overcome that ignorance.

Melody, aptly named, is waiting for the Holy Spirit to slap the ability to play the keyboard on her. She can play the violin but also has the desire to play the piano. Melody has not signed up for one piano lesson. I believe God, and I believe it can happen, but I don't necessarily believe Melody. There are many testimonies of the Holy Spirit moving on people to give them spiritual and natural gifts and talents instantly, when receiving salvation or in anointing services. But if time is passing and you still don't have the gift, skill, or talent, it could be a sign that you should be taking lessons or getting training in the desired field. Do it! Then God will bless your lessons and training supernaturally. If God hasn't truly promised Melody what she is planned for God to bless, then she may be very disappointed. *Brethren, I would not have you ignorant*. Melody will not sit before the praise team or choir Sunday as they minister by music. She cannot. There is nothing God can do with her as she is *ignorant* of how to play.

Others Who Are Money Thieves

- People working in jobs where they have no skill, experience, expertise, or intention of being productive.
- People who only show up at work on payday and you've found you can't give them their Friday pay before lunch because they won't come back until Monday or Tuesday.
- People who work above their intelligence skill and know-how.
  - I once had a realtor who couldn't read a city map. Couldn't give or understand street directions, couldn't find houses in the specified price range, or didn't want to. Once a desired home was found, she could check on its availability, but couldn't lead me to it. She didn't know any neighborhoods. Couldn't open the lock boxes on the house once I found it and led her to it.

Our relationship didn't last very long, yet this person who was a licensed realtor making 6% and commissions on the sale prices of the houses people found for themselves. If you are promoted past your interest, desire, or experience, you are not earning your paycheck, you are stealing it.

Also, people who describe their jobs as "helping" their employer. They don't deem that what they do is work; it's helping someone else, which usually means that they "help" when they feel like it. When they don't feel like "helping", they don't do any work, or are frequently absent from work.

Many of these helpers are actually ignorant of how to do their jobs. They don't identify themselves as part of the work team in that place of business, and therefore do not really "help" as they think they do. Employers are trying to assimilate a cohesive workforce, but these helpers are actually individuals hanging loosely off of teams or messing up what could be a **team**. This is still ignorance.

The Old Testament outlines a sin offering due to ignorance. Therefore, **ignorance must be a sin**. That's why God tells us to study to show ourselves approved. Haven't you ever heard the phrase, *As ignorant as sin?* Guess that came from the Bible.

Just because I personally was not going into the casinos or standing in the lottery lines myself, did not exempt me from the iniquity of the unclean use of my money that I had lent to the gambler. Even though the money was in the gambler's hand, it was my money. When my money, even lent money, went into bad places, bad things happened to the money I still had in my possession. So, when lending, ask the hard questions.

What ministries are you sowing into when you lend or give money to *individuals* instead of bringing it into the church? The money coming into the Church is intended for godly ministry and is *consecrated* to God. At least that money is being prayed over. What ministries are you enabling based on where your money goes, ministries of darkness or light? Blowing on dice and yelling, Big money, big money is NOT a prayer to God.

How are you earning your wages? Are you productive? Are you working as unto God? Are you honest on your job and are you taking care of another man's things? If you are, then God can bless you mightily.

When you notice that others that aren't doing what they're supposed to be doing and are seemingly getting away with it, does that irritate you? It sure does, and it's because we are **among some thieves**. We don't do what another man does. We do what God says do.

The Lenders

But love your enemies and do good and the land hoping for nothing again, and your reward shall be great, and ye shall be the children of the highest, for he's kind and to the UN thankful and to the evil, (Luke 6:35).

The Bible says we are to lend and not to borrow, (Deuteronomy 5:16). To be able to lend is a promise of God that we should appropriate. But how can you lend if you don't *have* to lend? If you don't have enough for your own needs with leftover abundance, then you are impoverished. Being able to lend is not only a promise, but also a blessing, and the blessings of Abraham shall be ours. We shouldn't consider them as options. Picking and choosing the ones we think we deserve. We don't *deserve* any of them. We shouldn't pick the ones we think we have enough faith for; this is not a grocery store where we choose things that we have enough money to buy. We should, to the glory of God, walk in **every** blessing and every promise--, else they are given in vain. If the birthday gift is not opened, then it is purchased and given in vain. If the birthright gift is not appropriated and used, is it also purchased and given in vain? Yes.

To be able to lend is a promise and a gift of God.

Not having enough to *lend*, is a curse of the law. Poverty is a curse of the law. You can read about the curses and Deuteronomy 28:16-68, but Galatians 3:13 tells us we are no longer under the Curse. Because of Redemption, we are able to lend. It is Scriptural and blessed to lend, but we are to be discerning and wise in our lending.

The New Testament says that we should lend hoping for nothing in return. The Scriptural significance of this is great as we read previously. If we *lend* we are still *attached* to the money, and indirectly connected to the path it travels, the consequences of where that money goes and what that money does. If we **give**, expecting nothing in return, we *release* ourselves from that money. I this way, we don't suffer in the consequences; we counted as dead. If and when this money returns to us after many days (Exodus 11:1), then it is not only a great surprise, but an incredible blessing to us again.

Have you, as a borrower ever heaped iniquity on the trusting lender by using the borrowed money for unclean use?

It is Scriptural and blessed to lend and to be able to lend. Pray that God will make you a lender which is under the blessing and not a borrower which is under the Curse. But when do you lend? If the situation fits in the spiritual laws and agrees with your spirit, then do it. If there is a check, hesitation, or if you are not really sure in your spirit, then seek God further before making the lending transaction.

One more important question, are you really *helping* the person? Or are you helping them to procrastinate about finishing school, developing a budget, becoming financially disciplined or getting a job? If you keep paying your unemployed son's car payment, what is his motivation for seeking employment? None. Lend only by acknowledging God first. Many people say you don't have to ask God about everything. The Scriptures say, *In all your ways acknowledge Him*, not in *some* of your ways.

Just Say No to Co-Signing

Cosigning is a form of lending. It is lending your name, reputation, credit rating and in cases of default, your checkbook or wallet to the individual for whom you are cosigning. It is a way that you purchase something that someone else has chosen for you to buy--, the car that they like, the color they like, the sports package they like. It could even be the house they like. Whatever it is, now that they have picked out something for you to buy, they make glowing promises or use other methods to cause you to sign your name on the purchase agreement.

If they default, then you pay. And if you pay, do you get the item? If it is repossessed, no one gets it. If it's not repossessed, then what happens to the item? Depends on the person. If they didn't pay the bank, then why would they turn the item over to you? And even if they did, would you even want it? Remember they picked it out, not you. They didn't keep their word to the bank and authoritative institution, what is to make you believe that they have suddenly become trustworthy and will keep their word to *you*?

Did Jesus cosign for anyone? Yes, everyone. And look what it cost Him. He gave it all, but He did it willingly. He was not tricked out of anything. **NO SIGN a CO-SIGN** unless you are able and prepared to pay it all. If you are asked to cosign for a car that costs $25,000, but you are not financially and emotionally prepared to pay the full $25,000 either in payments or all at once, then don't do it because you may have to. If you cosign, be prepared to *give* it.

Moneylending/Borrowing Prayer

Dear Heavenly Father, I praise You today for loading me with benefits. You are faithful and Provident. As You have given to me, I'm expected to give in return. Lord, I want to give cheerfully. I repent of all the bad decisions and wrong money choices I have made in stewardship in the past. I repent of any selfishness concerning money this day. I resolve to be obedient to Your Word, Your voice as You lead me to give, so it will be given unto me, pressed down, shaken together, and running over. From this day forward, I resolve to be faithful in my tithes and offerings, sanctifying it to the Kingdom of Heaven, thereby being a blessing and being blessed as well.

Lead me, Lord, by Your Word, Your teachings and anointed teachers placed in my path to know how to use wisely what You've entrusted to me. You said You give wisdom freely, Lord, to all who ask. Give me Wisdom and discernment, so I may know a Money Thief, a false borrower, and avoid deception.

Bless me, Lord, to be a lender, not a borrower, not because of bad credit or bad reputation, but by choice and by Your provision. Bless me, to be the head only and not the tail, to be above only and not beneath. Help me, Lord, to use the discernment You give me to lend only when appropriate and for appropriate causes.

Keep me by Your Holy Spirit from giving to liars, thieves, or to people who heap corruption in their own lives. Help me not to help people hurt themselves. Help me to see that if You've withheld money from them, I don't need to get involved.

Keep me from giving to people who sow to the flesh.

Keep me from sharing in the reaping of iniquity because of their sin.

And I repent of any unclean use of money, especially if I have caused iniquity to anyone who's lent me money or tried to help me.

I trust You, Lord, more than I trust money. I'm willing to give, share, donate, lend, and sow wherever You lead me by Your Spirit.

In the Name of Jesus, Amen.

CHAPTER FOUR

BLESSING THIEVES

-Not everyone is *named* Jacob.

Feeling helpless many times, saints often pray for power. We believers have power. It is hidden from the world, but it shouldn't be hidden from us. When we say, *No, we won't do that because of our God. We won't use or buy that, invest in, approve that or we won't bless that,* we exert our power. When we approve, validate, and condone actions and activities we bless. Giving a blessing takes power. When we bring correction in love or witness in the name of the Lord, we exert authority and exhibit power.

A pastor's wife befriended Jerome, a nice and likeable fellow. Jerome was living in overt sexual sin. The two worked together and had lunch together several times a week. He told her jokes that made her laugh. They became close friends, and after about three months, Jerome confessed his sin filled lifestyle to her, and waited for her response. Her response was no response.

They continue to be lunch buddies, although she made sure he didn't eat from her plate or drink from her glass again. If he tasted her ice cream, it became *his* ice cream, but they still were, *"friends"*.

Jerome wanted one of two things, correction and admonition, or the blessing. He probably, based on who she was, expected to be ministered to, have the law of God presented to him and the grace of God ministered to him. But he got **nothing**. And, saying nothing to Jerome about his lifestyle was the same to Jerome as giving a blessing. So, Jerome **received the blessing.**

Well, he'd boldly say, *She's a pastor's wife, if she didn't say anything about my lifestyle, if she can be my friend, then there must not be anything wrong with it.*

Their conversation even turned to her listening to his complaints about his sex life and many relationships. Perhaps her ears were itching, and she wanted to hear something trashy. Perhaps she just didn't have enough courage or boldness to counsel him. Worse, sadly, perhaps she did not have enough knowledge to witness to him or lead him in the Word.

Don't blame the Holy Spirit; she had not received the infilling of the Spirit at that time. But over the many months of their relationship, she could have studied and found the words to minister to him so God could set him free.

The blessing thief lurks. Silence is how the blessing can be stolen.

Yet another case of false blessing years ago and unmarried couple, each 19 years old, confessed to their pastor and his wife that they had had sexual relations, and we're now with child. The pastor's wife danced for joy that the young woman was having a baby. The pastor had no response. No one corrected the violations of holiness or fornication, and the young man who was a music minister was never sanctioned. There was no repentance, there was no marriage. Not that a wedding would make it right. And the young musician kept on ministering in the church. The choir gave the young woman a baby shower. Later, the pastor dedicated the baby—I mean really, it's not the baby's fault; the baby is not stealing the blessing. So, life, went on. No lessons were taught, no lessons were learned.

These young people were falsely "blessed" or became as Blessing Thieves when there was silence instead of boldness. They should have been corrected and led to repentance. Several years later, when the young man went to minister at an outside engagement, he proudly took his child with him. Many questions came up, such as we didn't know you were married. Where's your wedding ring? Where's your wife? Where's the baby's mother? The young man gave the true answers to all these queries because he had not been corrected, so he thought there was nothing wrong with the life he had developed for himself. He was never invited back to that church again, and quite a few other churches shunned him as well.

Money Mixing

Roy, who is unsaved, really knows how to make money and he wants you to go into business with him. He's been to Business School, and he has three other businesses, all very successful. Roy describes himself as a free spirit as his explanation for all the *unclean things* he does with his money. The question is, do you mix your money with his? Since you are bought with a price and Roy is not, ask God to direct you in this.

A Commandment to Bless

Ever notice how people who are about to do something wrong, recruit folk to do that wrong something with them? By doing something wrong with someone who is saved, and knows better, you are in essence, blessing them. In the Book of Numbers, Chapter 23, Balaam states that God has given **a commandment to bless**, and he, (Balaam) cannot reverse it. Balak hired Balaam to curse Israel, but Balaam could only bless. We are to bless one another in words, psalms, and hymns daily. We are to exhort, admonish, and minister to one another if one of us is doing something wrong, we may need the fellowship of another believer to correct us, or at least bring it to our attention. If one of us is about to drive down a road where the bridge is out, the other of us should tell him, not allowing him to drive down that road. The other of us should also not get in the car with that person and take that ride.

So, we have a commandment to bless, ability to bless, and authority by the Name of Jesus to bless others. A form of blessing is verbally approving another's actions.

Another way to say you approve of a person, or his plan is to put money on it. You invariably put your money where your mouth is, because out of the abundance of the heart the mouth speaks. When you invest in someone or their ideas, you bless them. By mixing your money with Roy's money to affect a business deal, you have in the natural, said to Roy, "I don't have any problems with you or your lifestyle and I'm willing to look past, ignore and/or participate in you continuing to make money, or even making more money."

In the spirit, since money is spiritual, you have said to GOD and any spiritual entity listening, "I approve of what you're doing, Roy and want you to make money so you can continue to live the lifestyle you now live and do whatever you want. I am willing to bring both money **and grace**, my spiritual reputation to the table to help Roy.

Now, Roy's money, and money-making skills help you. Roy is in the world's system; you are in the economy of God. You bring a lot more than cash to the table, but if Roy uses up all your grace before you get any or enough profits, then what? Then you begin to share in Roy's iniquity, for helping him make money for unclean use.

Do you mix your money with Roy? Perhaps if you're subject to backslide and begin to behave as Roy does, it's probably not a good idea to get into business with Roy. At the same time, this may be your best opportunity to witness to him, and it might be God's way of blessing you financially. Maybe. God hates unequal yokes, and business partnerships are like marriage. They are yokes

It's complicated, isn't it?

Every dollar is not from God, but that's another whole book. So, consider your true motive to getting involved with Roy. Is it to witness? Keep your motives pure so God can move in this situation.

If Roy wants you to invest in an *unclean* business, you wouldn't hesitate to say no. But is money used for ungodly use of concern to you when you help him make it?

You don't have to be a pastor or pastor's wife to **bless** by your deeds, actions, words, or money. You don't have to have a lot of money either; everyone blesses someone or something every day. By being Abraham's seed, you are blessed and charged to be a blessing. What you bless will affect you. Where your treasure is, there will your heart be (Matthew 6:21). An expression of your treasure is your money. Where you put your money will affect your Christian walk. Take it seriously and don't let a blessing be taken from you because of silence, or simply doing what everyone else is doing.

And remember: Every dollar is not a good dollar. And every dollar is not from God.

CHAPTER FIVE

SAINT THIEVES

Long ago, in a faraway country, there was a man who stole sheep. It didn't matter if they were black or white, he stole sheep. We don't know if he stole them for their wool or for spring lamb and mutton chops for meals, or both. After, not too long, the townspeople got wise to him and brought him to justice. His punishment was that on his forehead were brandished 2 letters S. T. which stood for sheep thief.

As most thieves are embarrassed when caught, he wore his hair as bangs over the brand for many years and many of the people forgot all about the sins of his youth. As genetics would have it, though, he began to bald and lost the ability to cover up the two letters S. T. He was then exposed again. The ridicule restarted. The former thief became weary of being ostracized even though he had changed his ways completely. The townspeople, especially the ones who were younger when this whole ordeal took place, could not see him in any other way than being a sheep thief. They disrespected him and teased him. When watching their own flocks, if they saw him pass along the road, they would not only not speak, but would herd their sheep to a remote part of the grasslands, as though he would, still, steal.

Wanting a better life, he moved from this town and found a new home hours and hours away where his former reputation, was not heard of. One day in his new town, he walked to the local market. A little boy who was shopping with his parents saw the reformed man and noticed the letters on his forehead. The boy asked his mother what did S. T. stand for, but she didn't know. Then he asked his father; but he also didn't know. Then the boy thought for a moment and said, I know, SAINT!

Thank God for salvation, restoration, and forgiveness from the sins of our youth. Thank God that He remembers our sin no more, and we can come into the House of the Lord for refuge and Sanctuary and lead the life God intended for us in the first place, without condemnation or scorn.

But everyone who comes into the House of the Lord is not saved and many *may not want to be saved.* How many stories have you heard of worldly, unsaved people seeking out a Christian spouse as a means of having a controllable wife or husband who won't cheat? These unsaved people have no intention or idea of loving their spouse as Christ loved the church, which is what the believing wife or husband expects. This can only lead to disaster and disappointment unless salvation is accepted by the unbeliever. If the Christian backslides, in an attempt to make the household more peaceful, that will not make a happy home; it might make it worse.

The Word says that any man who turns back is not fit for the Kingdom, so the believer can never stop serving God in order to please another; people pleasing does not work. (See Chapter One.) Don't let an unsaved spouse steal your joy and salvation. Don't let him or her steal your relationship with God.

> And Jesus said unto him. No, man, having put his hand to the plow and looking back, is fit for the Kingdom of God, (Luke 9:62).

Sheep Thieves

Christian men and women are in serious demand by many good and godly saints. Not only are they a commodity for Kingdom work, but they are wanted for personal and godly relationships. The world's statistics say that there are not enough men to go around. I believe that's an exaggeration.

The Christian woman is especially in demand. She is a commodity. Her price is far above rubies. He that finds her finds a good thing. She is the glory of her husband. Surely you don't think God only did that two-by-two thing for animals and livestock. Or do you think you'll have to wait until the next major flood to find a man?

There are countless worldly, short-skirt-wearing, no moral-having, do-anything women in the world who may be seeking relationships. She may be attractive to a man for a sinful season, but a man does not usually want to marry that kind of woman. Also, when it's marrying time, the worldly woman wants the worldly man to change, or she may also seek to marry a Christian man. You see, neither does the worldly woman want a worldly man when it's time to marry, even the worldly man doesn't want to marry the cosmopolitan woman either. So, he also steps into the Kingdom of God to *steal* a good Christian woman. Here, the letters S.T. come back again. This worldly person is a Saint Thief.

Oh, are you giggling? I hope you aren't. This is serious, the Christian woman unsuspectingly believes he is saved because he *said so*. Her discernment is nonexistent, or she ignores it. She may be turned by his natural good looks, charm, or worldly assets, or she may have made the decision to rebel against her own discernment, common sense, and her parents. Saint Thieves are not just out in the world, they may be sitting by you on the Pew. I have warned you, the Saint Thief is a wolf in sheep's clothing. But if you look closely, you'll see it's not even a good costume. Are those bell bottoms? His outfit is worn , wrinkled, and soiled. It has holes in it. Where has he been? That outfit is so thin, look there--, you can't help but see through it. He knows no Scriptures, but says he's been in church all his life. He doesn't know any praise music and knows parts to about two hymns. It's, a hymn, not, a hum. He wants the godly life, the Godly wife, a woman like his dear old mother, so he says. And he might actually mean it, but he doesn't know how to do it or how to live it.

Now is the right time to ask him about his mother and see for yourself how he treats her. Ask to meet her as soon as possible. She'll probably tell you the truth. Tracy dated one such fellow. The fellow's mother told Tracy, *"My son is a clever liar. He's no good. Get as far away from him as soon as possible."* Tracy did. And Tracy got away from that fellow's mother, too.

The Bible talks about Saint Thieves.

... In the last days, perilous times shall come.... Men shall be lovers of their own selves, covetous, boasters, proud, blasphemers, disobedient to parents, on, thankful, unholy without natural affection, trucebreakers false accusers and continent fierce. Despisers of those that are good traitors, heady high-minded lovers of pleasures more than lovers of God having a form of godliness... From such turn away, (2 Timothy 3:1-5).

Paul is telling Timothy about creeps, Saint Thieves. Those who creep into houses and lead silly women away into the doctrine of their own thinking, for their own purposes are creeps.

... they.. creep into houses and lead captive silly women laden with sins, led away with divers lusts, (2 Tim 3:6).

These men try to get *things* from women and try to get women to do whatever they want. Carol is a young professional Christian woman who recently had her expensive sports car stolen by her unsaved boyfriend. When she filed the police report, the officer stated very matter-of-factly, *"We get this kind of report all the time. I bet you go to church. Don't you, miss?"*

"Yes," she said.

"This is typical. A young professional woman, often a churchgoing woman, dating some guy from who knows where. He takes her car for days or weeks at a time. They're out there, ma'am, just looking and waiting for women like you."

There's Carol in a professional and possibly spiritual Promised Land, but still in the romantic wilderness. Why is she dating this unsaved man? What is it about Carol and or this man that keeps her attached to him? Look at yourself or your situation and ask these important questions. Is he the guy for you? Is she the woman for you? If so, can you bring that person home to meet your daddy? I mean your natural father **and** your Heavenly Father. If you have to apologize to God to present your significant other intended spouse, then he's not, she's not the one for you.

Wilderness Romances lead to Wilderness Marriages.

Yeah, there are bad ones out there, but every guy is not a jerk and, every girl is not an opportunist gold digger. Every guy is not a liar or thief, but it pays to be aware. Use discernment to be sure. When it comes to relationships, seek the counsel of parents, relatives, or saved and Spirit-filled friends who are in right relationship with God and in their own right, personal relationships. You may need to introduce this person to your church leaders and meet with your pastor or Christian marriage counselors. Bring him to church and let him meet the Elders. Let the men at the fellowship have a look at him. Then let the Church Mothers take a look at him, they are holy now, but they've been there, they've seen that. Whatever you do, don't just show up at church one Sunday morning, married to an unsaved stranger, because you couldn't help yourself, or he swept you off your feet. Build up your spirit so your flesh doesn't lead and destroy you.

And, be prepared to go to his church and meet all of those people too, so they can check you out for him.

The Man Shortage

That again.

There may not be enough good men to go around because both good women and bad women want good men. You know what I'm talking about. You've seen mismatched marriages yourself and probably wonder how did those two get together? Because the ways of a man are clean in his own sight, no matter how bad he or she is, they believe when it's time to get married that they should get the **best**.

You must guard against being stolen by a Saint Thief.

God knows what He's doing. He knows how to make a man and how to make a woman, and He knows how to count. Actually, if every woman came from the rib of a man, wouldn't there automatically be enough of each? There's no shortage of good men for good women, or vice versa. It's when worldly people see how fair the sons and daughters of God are and invade the Kingdom to steal Saints. That creates the discrepancy and available Christian men and women. They've been doing it since Genesis.

When a child of God is involved in a wrong relationship, he or she is blocking the work of God and causing problems with the right two getting together. That's why you should claim your God-made and God-given spouse right now. Pray for the God-chosen spouses for your children today.

PRAYER AGAINST SAINT STEALERS

Father, I worship You today because You made someone for everyone. For every man or woman that desires a spouse, you've made the suitable mate. I praise You, Lord, that we are not called to be alone, and that You put the solitary in families, (Psalms 68:6.) I bless Your Name, Lord.

Today I come against Saint Thieves, in the Name of Jesus. I come against wolves in sheep's clothing, (and other bad outfits), that they may have no place in the life and hearts of Your precious Saints. I pray that these thieves will be revealed and recognized by individuals in the Body of Christ. I pray that Your people will be wiser in avoiding marital mistakes, being taken advantage of, or having their time and resources wasted in wilderness relationships.

Help singles and even the widowed to meet their intended mates as is Your will. Destroy the work of the enemy so that true men and women of God will be yoked together according to Your Word, putting 10,000 to flight to Your glory Lord, to Your glory. Give them joy, peace and prosperity in their marriages and relationships. Lord, in the Name of Jesus, I ask You to uncover and unmask any wolves or Sheep Thieves that may be in my life, help me see them and know how to minister to them if they are to be witnessed to. Give me Wisdom, to know if to minister to them in words and testimony, or whether they are to be driven from the fold. Give me strength, Lord, to do Your will, in the Name of Jesus, Amen.

CHAPTER SIX

JOY THIEVES

Thou wilt show me the path of life; in thy presence is fullness of joy at thy right hand there are pleasures forevermore, (Psalms 16:11).

Joy is attractive. It's supposed to be. When people see it, they want it. However, if they don't fully understand, they may want *you* because they may think *you* are the reason for your own Joy. Many times, people may not understand that they can't take you away from the Source of your Joy and you still remain joyful. These are the Joy Thieves, and they fall into many categories.

- Some want to be around you because they are attracted to your Joy. They want and need Joy in their lives. You've heard the saying, *You can catch more flies with honey than vinegar.*

Remember when you didn't have Joy, you were so unattractive to people. You were vinegar then. Now that you have some Joy in you and in your life, you're like honey, Honey.

- Unfortunately, some want to be around you because they want **your** Joy or don't want you to have it. Those are kill-Joys.
- Others are clueless and are around you because of your Joy, but don't have any plans of stealing your joy, but if their sorrow or disappointment, depression, or heaviness outweighs your Joy, then they will in effect, become Joy Thieves.

Many joyless people know nothing about Joy, so when you are around them, you are responsible for possessing *your* joy. Do not let another who is joyless have any say so, or participation in your Joy. If you choose to share your Joy with them, that is your decision, but do not let another be in charge of your Joy--, except Jesus Christ because in His presence is fullness of Joy through the Holy Spirit, righteousness, peace, and Joy in the Holy Ghost.

Laura is saved and Spirit-filled. Her boyfriend adores her, but he wants to monopolize all of her time. She has quit the Praise Team, doesn't teach in Children's Church anymore, and she doesn't attend church fellowships. If you see her in church twice a month, it's a record. Laura has become miserable because she has not been in the *presence* of her Joy. Jose doesn't understand why she isn't nice and happy like she used to be. Jose was attracted to Laura's Joy and wanted Laura, not the source of her Joy, Jesus Christ. It's a form of idolatry where Jose thought *Laura* could bring *him* **Joy**.

Jesus is actually what he needs.

It is a common mistake women make thinking that a man can bring them Joy. Of course, it's described as *happy*. Happy is an external reflection of internal joy. In order to be happy you really need Joy. Just as the camera only takes what it sees, and a reflection can only be of what's in the mirror. **No Joy, no happy.** Happy without real joy is only an illusion. Most people are happy with things and money. Some place alcohol and drugs on their list of things that *simulate* happy.

If you meet a man or woman who is saved, dating, or marrying them won't get you saved. You've got to take some steps on your own. If you meet or marry a person because they have this attribute or that attribute doesn't mean you're going to get that quality unless you go through what they went through or something similar to get it. Even if it's Joy, you can't get it *from* them, you can only get it from the place they got it--, Jesus. You get it by any of the processes by which they got it: Salvation, Discipline, Knowledge, Wisdom, Praise and Worship.

No matter how much you admire the good fruit in others, you've got to take steps to get your own. Being covetous and trying to take theirs will not do you or them any good. Go to the Source, Jesus Christ.

Why? Because your Joy is made just for you. People can steal your Joy and can trade it, or even give it away, but your Joy may not do the next guy any good. Your Joy is tailor-made and custom-designed just for you. What brings you pleasure, and joy may not do a thing for someone else. What brings them joy may not do anything for you. So, possess your joy; don't let it go.

Conversely, your hell or sorrow is also custom designed for you. My mother used to describe nightclubs and bars as *hellholes*. If you're a party animal or an alcoholic, you might not think that hell is so bad if a bar is a hellhole. But hell is not a place where you can indulge your fantasies or assuage your flesh. Hell is all the things you fear, all the things you hate and all the things you abhor. It is all the things that worry, disgust, or sadden you. What's in Hell are all the things that make you sick and things you definitely don't want to see, hear, or do. Hell will be custom made just for you. What's *hell* to you may not be held to me.

Hell to a demon is living in the presence of the Holy Spirit. You know that Light that you are letting shine in your home because you just can't help it? That Light is wearing that evil, Joy-killing, Joy-thieving *spirit* out. But that's just who's trying to ZAP your Joy by trying to quench your prayers, your praise, your worship, and the Spirit of God that's in you. It's completely wearing that demon out.

To me, being in the presence of God, being filled with the Holy Spirit is *Heaven*. Your unsaved mate/spouse may not find that very enjoyable. Unsaved mates are common Joy-killers and Joy Thieves. They are jealous of God and/or church. That abiding Joy that you have may just be what they desperately want and need. But they don't have it, don't know how to get it, and don't want you to have it either. Looking only in the natural, they may have made statements, or given ultimatums such as, *"Either that church or me."* Or their approach may be more benign, *Honey would you like to go to brunch this Sunday or take a weekend trip?*

True, you may have married him in the Romance Wilderness, but somehow you have made it to the Promised Land. For that, you are so thankful. But your mate is still the outdoorsman--, he is still in the Wilderness and enjoying the view.

The Joy or the Job?

Your boss wants you to work Sundays all of a sudden, and you've been told come to work, *or else*. Or more subtly, you've been asked to work Sunday for *double time* or **triple time**. Is that all it takes to get you to stop coming to church, $100? That's not saying much about what you think of God. Anything that wants to take you out of His Presence is a Joy Thief.

Possess Your Soul!

In your patience possess ye your souls, (Luke 21:19).

Possess your souls means to possess your mind, your will, and your emotions. As Joy is an emotion, you must possess your Joy. That means even as deliberate, or unintentional Joy Thieves approach you, you must decide that the Joy you have is yours, and you want to walk in it. Just as when anybody gets anything attractive, people come up to it. Fruits of the Spirit such as Joy are supposed to be attractive to people, but they can also attract flies. So, you must grow this fruit, prosper in this fruit, share this fruit, when necessary, *yet possess it*, and keep the flies off of it. All to the praise of His Glory.

PRAYER FOR JOY

Lord, You are the Source of my strength, and the Joy of the Lord is mine by covenant. Lord, I adore You, I worship You. I bless Your Name. You're awesome, and You are Holy. I will, Lord, in the Name of Jesus, to possess my soul. I will possess my emotions, my will, and my intellect. I strive to become more like You every day, in the Name of Jesus. I purpose to minister to those to whom I should, and I purpose to maintain and possess my Joy. I cultivate Joy by being in Your Presence and entering into worship. I will and I purpose to allow no other than You to affect my Joy and its reflection--, happiness as I walk as a Christian, should. It's all to the glory of God and in the Name of Jesus, Amen.

CHAPTER SEVEN

KNOCK-KNOCK

Verily, verily, I say unto you, he that entereth not by the door into the fold of the sheep, but climbing up some other way, the same as the thief and the robber, (John 10:1).

A note came across the Fax the other day. It was a dear note, very personal and signed by a person with only one initial. Cher has one name, and many other people may have one name. Some people only use their initials, there are JB's and JR's, for example. The artist formerly known as, only has symbols-- ironically, the symbols similar to those that cartoonists used to express expletives. Anyway, the author of this particular Fax only had one alphabet which by which I should recognize them. Guess who? Must I? No. Why can't you sign your name? Why use initials or an alias? Are you embarrassed about who you are, or what you wrote? Or is there something going on that shouldn't be going on? I couldn't receive the note. Just as a guess-who telephone call would be a goodbye phone call, so goes the Fax.

Children and adolescents play the Guess-Who game, but it is not becoming to adults, especially those who are supposed to be on the up and up. And the behavior is certainly not becoming to Christians. Did Jesus say, *Guess who?* When He asked the Disciples, **"Who do men say that I am?"**(Mark 8:27) No. He inquired about His reputation in the land. We know this because He had already and continued to tell the Disciples who He was.

Jesus is our model.

Back Door People

The sheepfold only had one door. The Word says that anyone who comes into the fold in any other way except through that door is a thief and a robber. Katie said goodnight and left the reception. Then a half an hour later she was back at the gathering, seated beside someone else's husband. She must have come in through the back door when someone else wasn't looking. Why? What's the big deal, Katie? The sad thing is, I'm talking about church folk. Least of all should these things be happening in the House of God and among so-called Saints of God. Anyone who does not come in through the door is a thief, a robber, and add liar to that too.

But there are multifaceted people-- I mean, multi-faced people. They smile in your face, as the saying goes, but all the time they have another agenda completely. Sandra became best friends with Pat because she wants to spend time with Pat's fiancé.

Sandra claims the "Lord" told her that Pat's fiancé was to be Sandra's husband. I'm always amazed at that. If God doesn't reveal to *both* parties that they are to be married, if God can't reveal to *both* parties, then they must be on different spiritual levels. And if that is the case, they will be unequally yoked.

I have a question especially for the ladies. Why is it that so many women confess that God has shown them their husband, but I've never heard one man say that God has shown him his wife and ask when or if he should tell her. Yes, God does talk to all of us, but is he talking to brides more than grooms? Somehow, I don't think so.

God made Adam first. Then, communed with him. Especially with the predominance of male ministers that there are in the world, I believe the male gender is quite capable of hearing from God, especially in matters as serious as their own spouse.

Carla was so convinced that the Lord had shown her that a certain young man was to be her husband, that she spent several years trying to win the man. When she told the fellow of "God's" revelation to her, she scared him half to death. As far as I know, the man is still running, which is a hard thing to do while half dead. At least Carla and this gentleman were friends. Often, I've seen women point out their husbands-to-be in crowds, in a congregation, or even on television. These **pre-husbands** not only do not know that these "wives" exist, but they also have no way of meeting them. Least of all do these men expect that they are the object of allegedly divinely arranged marriages.

Abraham sent his servant to get Rebecca for Isaac. David sent for Bathsheba, then later married her. **Where in the Bible has a woman sent for a man to be her husband? I haven't found it.** Women, don't blame your strong fleshly desires on God. And don't be sneaky. There's a genre of 60s and other films that show *how the woman got her, man*. I'm sure these movies were intended for entertainment only. Take a warning if you grew up watching stuff, please-- this is not God's way; these are movies.

Game playing and deception are devilish behavior and tactics.

God is not the one putting these marriages together, man is. What God puts together; no man can put asunder. God does not put marriages together with lies and deception. Wait on the Lord.

Reading from Genesis, the woman is first *prepared* and **presented** to the man, not the other way around. Esther was ***prepared*** for months before entering the king's court. If God has a man for you, and I believe he does, if He said so, now is your *preparation time*, spiritually, financially, physically, and emotionally. God will tell the man too--, maybe even first, maybe *only*. Then the man will come to you, Lady Saint, decently and in order. God will not slip, sneak, or hide. Telling just one person of a pair so they can set out on a spouse-getting mission is rather cruel, wouldn't you say? God is not cruel.

Just as men are made to be hunters and pursue, women should be the object of a man's desire and she should *be pursued*. How will you reconcile this if **you've** chased *him*? He still has to get his desire to pursue women out of him. Shouldn't it be with you, as his wife? God knows His creation and He knows men do not like to be overly pursued. Men feel trapped if they haven't been the initiator, or at least a consenting party in a major, and hopefully prayerfully, permanent relationship.

It's Our Secret, Don't Tell Anyone

You learned about that in kindergarten. Anybody who couldn't say it in front of everybody or at least somebody else, shouldn't say it at all. If you have to whisper, you didn't need to say it. The Don't-Tell-Anyone's were usually gossipers, perverts, and sexual deviants. **It's Our Secret** is not only their name and their label, but also their mantra. You were taught to stay away from those characters. So, it goes now that you're grown up in church, you should even keep an eye on church leaders, or would-be church leaders who give assignments in private.

Beware. Every Saint, *ain't*.

And you know that secret prophecy is a no-no. If someone has to take you to a parking lot or a corner of the church to share what they say is a, "thus saith the Lord" concerning you, be suspicious. The person may actually mean well, but they may be a spiritual deviant who is under the *spirit of error, a lying spirit,* or a *spirit of false prophecy*, or *divination*. Receive the word that God has for you in public so that it can be judged. If God only wanted **you** to know, He'd tell you Himself. Share the "prophecy" you have received with your Deacon, Pastor, prophetic team, or church Spiritual Prophecy authority.

When you believe you have a Word from the Lord, see your pastor first to receive permission to share it. If you don't have boldness to speak it--, let's recall that boldness was the first thing that the people received on the day of Pentecost, even before the spiritual gifts were doled out. They all spoke with boldness. If you don't have a knowing, a certainty, and a **boldness**, is it indeed from God?

Boldness was the first gift at Pentecost.

Avoiding Proper Channels

Unless people have severe shame or self-esteem issues, secrets and evasive behavior should not be commonplace. If they have phobias and fears connected with rejection, then it may be understandable that they may use unorthodox methods in attempting to have relationships or communicating with others--, for a time. But we shouldn't help them stay dysfunctional. The normal person, which is described by psychologists, is 80% of the population, should not behave this way. Do your friends behave this way? Do you? You may be 100% innocent and guilt free, but you may be perceived as a thief, a robber, or a liar, especially if you are one of those who cannot look another in the eye.

Behold, I stand at the door knock if any man hear my voice and open the door, I will come into him. And will Sup with him and he with me, (Revelations 3:20).

Jesus is still our model and He, in the above passage stands at the door and knocks. He doesn't crawl or climb up to a window and peek in to surmise what's going on. He doesn't climb in through the window. He doesn't go around the back and try the lock. He doesn't just stand outside of a closed door, for instance, and eavesdrop. He certainly doesn't climb up on the roof and shimmy down with chimney. (There goes that lie.) Neither is rudeness or unmitigated gall, boldness. Jesus stands at the door and knocks.

Knock, knock.

"Who's there? Thank you for knocking. It shows you have good manners. Hopefully God manners." Then Jesus, the only Supermodel, waits to be invited in, to come in and sup.

Jesus doesn't send suspicious messages by people. That's why there's no secret prophecy. God's messages that come through the prophets are to admonish, exhort, comfort, and edify. Most of God's prophets in the Old and New Testaments stood in the assembly, often risking their lives, and proclaimed what *thus saith the Lord*. God doesn't send cryptic messages with no signature.

Sometimes the signature is His Voice but His Voice is a signature that we should know. He doesn't send messages with just an initial: Love you, G.

God doesn't get your attention to ask, *Guess who?* We may, depending on our relationship with Him, be asking, *Who?*, but that's our fault. God is straightforward.

Now you know what the full armor of Ephesians 6:20 is for; it's for life's situations. When you find yourself **among some thieves**, among some robbers or among some liars. You should go to church, but you can't just hide in church. Why? Because you know who's in church? Regular folks. You're going to have to put on and use that armor at some time or other. Use your God- given discernment, use your common sense, and heed wise counsel from wise people. Folks who don't present correctly usually do have something to hide. People who don't have a last name or a whole name, people who can't come to see you during business hours, but they want a favor, or people who don't follow the proper channels all can be suspect. Those who send you notes to ask, *Will you please see me?* are all included. It's childish at best, worse dysfunctional, and demonic at the very worst.

The thief comes not but for to steal, kill and destroy. One way you can recognize him is by his knock, if he has one.

But the more sophisticated thief may actually come with a knock-knock.

"Who's there?" you say.

If you hear nothing or you hear a code name and alphabet or some symbols. Beware.

CHAPTER EIGHT

YOUR IDEA, THE OTHER GUY'S PROMOTION

When it comes to inspired ideas from Heaven, God releases all good (not evil) ideas onto the Earth. Since there is nothing new under the Sun, God is the only one who has profitable, new ideas. A concept or inspiration comes from the spirit realm and then into the consciousness of several, maybe even many people at the same time. Take, for instance, revelation of Scripture, many preachers across the country may have the same or similar message at the same time. They're not copying each other necessarily; they may not even know each other. That's God.

In our church, many report going to conferences and hearing the same message is our pastor has recently ministered. That's God. He knows what He wants His people to hear.

More than a dozen years ago, I thought that it surely would be nice to have one almond in a

Hershey's kiss. I had thought this early one morning when I had just awakened. Believing it was a dream about a TV commercial, I thought no more of it for a while, but I looked for the new item every now and again in the grocery store. Several years later, I was much surprised to find it hadn't been a dream at all. Thirteen years ago (before the writing of this book), the one almond in a Kiss didn't yet exist. It was a new idea that I had received in my consciousness. I don't know, but perhaps 12 or 13 years ago was the same time the person who worked for the Hershey, or the person who sold the idea to Hershey received the same idea.

Scriptures tell us that it rains on the just and the unjust alike, (Matthew 5:45). So, who decides who writes a symphony, or a great book, or patents a great idea or revolutionary invention? Why don't only God's people get all the new inventions or own all the patents? Who decides? Is it God? Or maybe the question should be is it God, *alone*? If He has just dropped the same idea onto the planet and several people have received it, what happens next?

The person who acts in Faith first will have the success. Jesus told the Roman Centurion that he had not seen greater faith in all of Israel, (Luke, 7:9), then He honored his faith by healing the Roman's servant. This Centurion was not even saved, so it shows that

101

God will honor **faith**. If you are not moving in faith, someone else may receive the blessings God intended for you, even if they aren't saved.

So now you have an idea what are you planning to do? Are you just going to talk about it? Tell it to naysayers? Tell it to family or friends? Or tell it to people who've been there, who've done that, and will accept responsibility to assist you? Why not tell it to people like patent attorneys, and marketing professionals that you have retained to bring your idea to market? Or tell people such as professional artists who will draw up your idea. You may need to plan with people such as chemists or businessmen and bankers who will assist you, and in doing so they will reap benefits in their own field. You show that you're acting in faith when you contract with people who will help you bring your ideas and plans to fruition.

Or will you tell it to your best friend while complaining about how you wish you had the resources to make it into a business or a profitable idea? Will you tell it to a coworker over lunch, trusting that you are speaking in confidence? Then, weeks later, find that coworker just received a promotion for coming up with a new way to make money for, or save the company time-- using *your idea*!

Then you may be accusing God asking Him, how could **He** let this happen to you? Rick Johnson started in the mailroom with you two years ago, and now he's your supervisor. How could *God* allow this? Rick is not even as smart as you are. Or is he? If faith pleases God, then having, using, and building your faith is smart.

A dental laboratory technician shared a new lab technique he had developed with a dentist friend. The dentist was so impressed with it that he called a patent attorney and now has a new product patented on the market in the dentist's name only. The laboratory tech has not and will not receive any of the glory or profits from his own God-given invention.

How could *God* let this happen? God didn't *let* it happen. You, after receiving the idea, have to set your mind like a flint and set your hands to the task. Move in faith to bring your promise forth. Stay prayerful. Get Wisdom. Use Wisdom when talking about it. Don't give the idea away to others.

God gives divine and inspired ideas, whether it's something brand new or a better way to do something old, what we do next depends on Wisdom and faith. Wisdom is the correct application of knowledge, and we know that faith from Hebrews 11:1 is **NOW**. If God is giving you a good idea, then act on it now. If has picked you, Praise Him! Know that you may be **among some idea thieves**, but don't give your gifts and ideas away.

Inspired Ideas Prayer

Dear Heavenly Father, You are the Creator of Heaven and Earth. There's nothing new under the Sun. All good gifts come from You. All new things come from You. You said in Your Word, *"Behold, I do a new thing,"* (Isaiah 43).

Thank You, Lord, for giving us new and inspired ideas. Thank You, Lord, for trusting us with Revelation knowledge. Thank You, Lord, for opening the Heaven over us and pouring out by Your Spirit God-ideas inspired thoughts and blessings.

Lead us by Your Spirit, to use Wisdom and faith to make the God-ideas entrusted to us realities that manifest in the Earth to bless the people that you intend to be blessed. We pray that the recipient of a God idea will be blessed, the Kingdom of God will be blessed and that the people that use the product or invention or a new way of doing things may be blessed. Guard us from the *idea thieves* let Your people be blessed, in the Name of Jesus. Amen.

CHAPTER NINE

SO, YOU USED TO OWN SOME *STUFF*?

Barbara phoned her husband from work to ask if he had finished mowing the lawn, as he had promised.

"I can't do that, honey."

"Why not? Is the mower broken?"

"No, it's not here."

"Where is it?"

"I lent it to my sister."

"Right, she borrowed it, but that was last month."

"She hasn't brought it back yet."

"Does your sister ever return anything that she so-called borrows?"

Did you use to own stuff that you no longer own? Whether it's a garden tool, a cup of sugar, or an umbrella--, it's stuff that you owned on Monday and on Tuesday that you may have wanted to use

Wednesday or at least plan to still own it next week, but you no longer own it. You may not even know who's got it, where it is, or if you'll ever see it again. Gladly you would have given them the item, but they only asked to use or borrow it.

What does the Bible say about giving? Where does the term give until it hurts come from, not from Scripture. The cheerful giver doesn't **hurt**. The widow's mite, the widow at Zarephath, kind of bet those two widows were already hurting, so they most likely gave to keep from continuing to hurt.

Abraham gave 10% of all; nobody made him, so that didn't **hurt**. God asks for the same 10% as our tithes, but not to hurt us. It's to bless us. One hundred percent (100%) would hurt many of us, like the first church after the day of Pentecost, (Acts 2). Thankfully, God doesn't ask that of us.

But God has asked that we give something of value. In essence, Jesus was the first person to say, *Show Me the money*, (Matthew 22:17). Then Paul said that if we give to you of our spiritual things, then you can give of your carnal, worldly things. The offerings in the Bible were things like the first fruit, the first crop, or a bullock. In Bible days to offer a bullock was more than a smelly piece of livestock. It was to be the best bullock or the fatted calf. We are to give things of value.

Thieves may be lurking to borrow things that you have. There are covetous, envious, and strife-filled folks, but the things you have, whether gifts or things you've worked for are for purposes other than being stolen from you. The things you have should be organized for use:

- Those things pertaining to life.
- Those things pertaining to godliness. These are things used for your spirituality, worship, sacrifice, tithes, offerings, alms, charity, and your ministry.

You may not put up much of a struggle when the things that pertain to life are threatened, or maybe you will, but what about a thief who tries to steal those things that pertain to godliness? If you allow something you need for your life to be stolen from you, shame on you. If you allow something you need for your godliness to be stolen, such as money, anointing, gifts, talents, treasury, or dedicated items, then, shame on you again.

There is an intersection of those things you need for life and godliness. Where is it? Depends on who you are, how you worship and what's important to you. Most people think it's only money, but that's not always true. If your blue shoes are borrowed and never return to you, you'll make do by wearing the black ones. But what if something you need for godliness was taken away? What will you use then? What will you offer to God if your sacrifice is stolen? What if your praise, your Joy, or you're offering were stolen? How do you regain it? People covet others' offerings. Cain started it by coveting Abel's offering. It's when you are really honoring God that your life and godliness completely overlap.

Have you ever had a present sent back to you? Doesn't feel too good, does it? Can God accept your offering? He didn't accept Cain's. If you have not given your best, God may not *receive* it. If your best has been stolen from you, if you don't have it, second best will be rejected.

God requires the offering for sin, for atonement, and for peace. He asked for certain kinds of offerings. He reserves the right to accept it or reject it. Can you imagine how Cain may have felt having his gift sent back? You don't want that to happen between you and God, right?

God deserves the best. He asked for and expects the best. The firstlings of the flock, for example. So, when the best bullock was sacrificed, they gave much more than just an animal. Livestock in those days may have represented any or all of the following to them.:

- Sacrifice they knew to bring a quality sacrifice.
- Sustenance.
- Family pet. Growing up on a farm, my sister, Angie named the livestock. Now she's a vegetarian.
- Food.
- Livelihood.
- Wealth.
- Transportation. These were nomadic people.
- Agricultural means. Produce.
- Clothing. Leather, fur.
- Marriage. Dowries bargaining chip, no pun intended.
- Worship. They could not worship without their livestock. Today, that is the equivalent of coming to church without our wallets. There is no worship in that.

The people did not worship without their livestock; the people did not worship without their OFFERINGS. Moses asked Pharaoh if the people could take their cattle and go worship. Pharaoh said, "No," so they didn't go. And they didn't worship without their children. Take a hint, modern day saints.

Did you know that an average bullock or cow can fetch big dollars on the market today, upwards of $1000 or more? In the early days before refrigeration, one bullock could feed a whole community for days. Many years later, when meat was salted down for preservation, it could feed the community even longer. But the best bullock was the expected offering, or the fatted calf, the veal. You know how much veal costs in the grocery store and in restaurants? We're not talking about shabby sacrifices because we are not talking about a shabby God. If you ask God for something, He sends the best, right? Yes, not mediocre. Not the worst, but the best, right? In the Old Testament people gave the equivalent of a month's salary or more for their offering. **Joyfully**. We should pay our tithes of 10% with joy, to the Most High and give our offerings, with gladness to honor God.

Neither was the animal sacrifice to become a pork roast or a cookout. The sacrificial meat was sacred and not to be eaten. It was holy unto the Lord. A true sacrifice was given and then not touched again, just as our gifts should be counted as God's, once given. Only the priest could partake of a portion of it. But the event was not for flesh indulgence.

Among other things, if God asks for you for 25% or 50% of your salary, what would you do? What if you really were called to be a slave? What if God required 100% of your earnings? As a slave to the world, you spent all of your money pursuing things and stuff. What did the Hebrews do about slavery in Egypt? They got out of there. We should do the same. Get out of slavery to the world and its pursuit of stuff.

Thankfully, God does not require **all**, as the Egyptians required of the Hebrews in Egypt.

We are on God's Earth working His land. We are not sharecroppers. So, God does not require an exorbitant amount of us, just 10%.

God says we are to give. To *give* means to share, or to yield under pressure. Which are you doing? We are not supposed to give away all our possessions to people who *borrow* them. We are not to give away our God ideas. We are to obey God's Laws and principles. If you give to share, that blesses others as well as yourself. If you yield under pressure, like a doormat, that doesn't bless you or the person who took it from you.

We can pay tithes and give offerings in the House of God, or we can be tricked out of it in the world. The Devourer roams about seeking to steal stuff you have, if you're not tithing. The Devourer is the one who has all the stuff you used to own. It should be evident to you that we are *among some thieves.*

In our giving. We are to give something of value, but don't let it be stolen from you by thieves.

Be wise stewards.

CHAPTER TEN

BABYSITTING:

LIVE-IN'S & DROP-OFFS

--If you have to check for stretch marks, it's not your kid.

You've already bought your children's school clothes and registered them for school. Sam will be in the third grade this year, Terri, the 5th. They're lovely children, but you don't have any baby pictures of them on the mantle. You don't have a medical record or their vaccinations, and you don't have any pictures of you while pregnant with them. *Oh, it's because they're not your children. They belong to your sister.*

Thinking back, you recall seeing your sister once this summer, around Memorial Day. She came over, dropped the kids off, and asked if they could stay the weekend because they just love Aunti Emm.

But now it's August.

You rifle through your important papers to see if you claimed these children on last year's tax returns. No. One last check--, your abdomen--, for stretch mark, . No stretch marks, and no recollection of morning sickness; it's conclusive, these are someone else's kids.

Let's see. You think aloud. *My sister and her husband were taking a weekend vacation to the Poconos. How could time have passed so quickly?*

Homemade Father's Day cards on the coffee table addressed to you and your husband. And they're from *these* children. *What's going on here?*

"Sam, Terri!" you yell out. The children are precious, they're obedient, clean, neatly dressed. They should be, you dressed them. They are cute and polite. And who wouldn't want these two around?

"Kids, we've gotta talk," you hesitate, *"about your parents. Have you seen your parents?"* The kids seem confused. *"When did you last talk to your parents?"* They looked at each other and giggle.

You insist, *"When are your parents coming to get you?"*

The two burst out laughing, exclaiming, *"You're so funny, Mom."*

Sam calling you, Mom really tugged at your heartstrings. You choked back a tear. *"Go play, kids. I have to lie down."*

You take a restless nap. You get up and take out your telephone to call your sister. Let's see, what is her new last name? What are the last names of the kids? Oh yes, Smith. You call. It's voice mail.

You leave a message, *"This is me; call me as soon as you get this message."*

There may arise occasions in every family where children stay with relatives for extended periods.

- Planned vacations.
- Sleep overs.
- Illnesses.
- The passing of a relative.
- Other family emergencies.

The Bible teaches not to wear at our welcome, (Proverbs 25:17). Parents, that means your kids too.

Train Up a Child

And we are admonished to train up a child, (Proverbs 22:6). If you, the parents, are not training up the child that God has blessed you with, then you are not in line with Bible teaching.

I believe that God sends the parent the exact child to grow the parent and the child up--, usually a child, just like them. God sends the exact child to highlight, reflect and mirror the stuff in you that He wants to show up, the praise as well as the flaws.

114

There are extenuating circumstances, but for the most part I believe this is God's plan.

The Lord will perfect that, which concerns me. Thy mercy, O Lord endureth forever, forsake not the works of thine own hands, (Psalms 138:8).

God sends people to help perfect that which concerns you. Parents, your children may even be a part of that *perfecting* process.

If your nieces and nephews are over at your house, how is that helping your sister or brother? Is it helping them to get to work on time, or get that college degree that they stop trying to get 10 years ago because they wanted to work and buy a new car? Is it helping them to *relax* or *enjoy themselves* because they never have any time to themselves? And how is that helping **your** children? Sure, the kids maybe having fun right now playing with their little cousins, but will they later grow up to be resentful of them for having to share their mom and dad?

And how about you? What is your sister or brother really doing while you're babysitting for days, weeks or possibly months at a time?

Parents, unfortunately, abandon children every day of the week, many for very selfish reasons. Most often because there's a relative or friend who will take care of their child for them while they do whatever activity that they want to do that does not include their children. Enabling your adult relatives who have children to be free to do whatever they want to do, as though they are still single, usually does not really help anybody. Often, they are involved in dangerous and unproductive behavior, or they would take their children with them.

Nate is a father who said he would never go anywhere where he could not take his child. And as the old joke goes, when he's judged, he will get the finest of cars to drive around in Heaven for all eternity. (Ask your pastor.)

So, you want your sister or brother to stop partying, become more disciplined, and grow up? What's the motivation for the natural parents to grow up if their kids are taken care of and they have no responsibility? In Malachi 4, God says He will turn the hearts of the fathers back to the children. That's God's order. God knew that they would be turned away from one another. If you're helping the adults remain just as they have always been, that cannot be good for the family or pleasing to God. Evaluate if you're really helping in the long term; be honest. Might you also be potentially damaging yourself while trying to help your family?

Are you attempting to cover up the bad behavior of a sib because you don't want it to get out, that they need help? That's risky business too. When will they ever get help? Look at these scenarios.

Scenario 1. Your sibling or friend's child grows up in your care and becomes successful.

All of a sudden, delinquent parents will become model parents. They begin to reap the benefits of the seed you sowed in rearing their child. What parent wouldn't run to parents' night to watch their boy, quarterback varsity football as captain of the team, or, their daughter speak as college valedictorian? You want this for the child you've raised or helped raise, right?

What about you? Where are you while all this is happening? Are you even invited? I'm not suggesting that any of us do any of these things for glory.

A woman who helped a teen during four years of college because her parents wouldn't. Now the child is finished school and doesn't even speak to the woman because her unsaved parents *don't like* the child's benefactor.

Scenario 2. Child grows up, gets in trouble. It's your fault.

Folk just won't know what you taught the child. She should have stayed with her mother. And you will be the bad guy, even after all the sacrifices you have made.

Scenario 3. Child grows up and resents you for trying to discipline him or her. You may hear retorts, such as, *"You're not my mother or father."* Or the popular vernacular, *"You ain't none of my momma or daddy."*

All the while, family and onlookers accuse you of stealing or trying to steal your sib's children, for whatever reasons, when you were only trying to help Outsiders and naysayers will look for motives, and they will find them even if they have to fabricate them:

- Money child may get a check of some kind, a death benefit or trust fund.
- Clean your house, cut grass, or serve you and your family in some capacity.

In reality, if you're a *real* Christian, the child in your home is more likely to be treated as a guest or noticeably better than your own children. At least your natural children may have this observation.

- Babysit your younger children.

Somehow it will either appear or be made to appear that *you* are benefiting by having a child in your home. Even foster parents are accused of keeping kids *for the money*. It may be true to a degree, but have you ever tried to feed a growing child or teenager? How many parents have you ever met who have **more** money now that they have children? What, are the children secretly working for the daycare where you send them, babysitting the daycare workers and the daycare workers pay the kids? Oh please! Are the parents getting checks *from* the daycare center for taking their child there? Of course not.

A benevolent couple kept a relative's child during his infant and toddler years. The child received a trust fund check, had nearly $500 per month. To prove to the family that the child's money was not being stolen and misused, the couple endeavored to save the trust fund money for the child. Daycare for the infant was $525 per month. Add in the cost of clothing, food and other supplies for the child and you will quickly realize if you haven't already, that having and raising a child is not a **money-making** venture. It costs a couple nearly $1200.dollars per month of their own money while saving the child's check. Yet, they were still looked at with ungrateful and accusing eyes.

Raising a child is not a money-making venture.

For the above reasons, I recommend the three-night rule. If there is emergency, you and your children can stay three nights. After that, other arrangements must be made. You may agree to stretch it to seven nights or one month, in extreme cases.

Harboring unhappy relatives and strangers may be your ministry. Neither am I trying to diminish the gift of hospitality if you have it. Whatever you decide just to establish it clearly before doing anything, write it down if you have to; the generational curse of amnesia may run in your family.

Families should stick together, but not at the expense of one for the benefit of all the others.

BABYSITTING PRAYER

Dear Heavenly Father, thank You for giving us the gift of children. Thank You for giving us the gift of family. We bless You, Lord for You are the Father of us all. You're the Lord of our life. You are our all in all.

Thank You for the gift of life from our own bodies. As new life comes forth through us, we thank You for guiding us, keeping us in loving us. Thank You for giving us a quiver full for blessing the fruit of our loins. Praise You, Lord, for the blessing of children.

Thank You, Lord, for family, for sisters and brothers, who also are given the gift of children and thank you for friends and loved ones who have children. Lord, we desire to minister to those whom you place in our life. We desire to bless them, all to Your glory. Lord, give us Wisdom to know the right time to minister to a little one and for what season help us to have compassionate hearts toward the needs of others, but not to be used or trampled on.

Be the Lord of our Lives. Be the Lord of our Wisdom. Let us be like You, Lord in the giving of ourselves, our time, and our hearts to children who may not have come from our loins.

Help us to be a blessing to the mothers and fathers who have given birth to natural children yet are unaware as to how to, or unable to care for their children, in the Name of Jesus. You decide, Lord whose child I should minister to, at what level and what season, and for how long. I trust You, Lord, and I'm willing, in the Name of Jesus. Amen.

CHAPTER ELEVEN

WHINING, BEGGING, PLEADING, GUILT & LYING

If you find you get emotional or are prone to do things that you are later sorry about, then the phrase, *Just don't do it,* may not work for you. This chapter may help you when someone presents you with a question or dilemma. What would you do if there were no guilt applied? If you feel compelled or confused when presented with hard decisions, seek counsel from wise, experienced, Spirit-filled people. Ask counsel of your church deacons, leaders, elders, or your pastor.

Ask yourself if you'd do what's being asked if the person, child, or child-like person didn't whine? If the person didn't beg or plead, would you do it? If the answer is no, then under the emotional duress of whining, begging, pleading and being made to feel guilty, isn't the answer still, *No?*

Whining, Begging & Pleading

Psychologists say that a child stops growing at the age he or she masters getting things they want, often that's the whining stage. That's why so many adults still whine. What would you be willing to do to get a child or adult to stop whining? Almost anything? I bet whining moves many people to give in. As annoying as it is, you must be strong not to give in just because a person is whining. You're being tricked emotionally, and they are not growing at all.

Mattie, who's in her middle 60s, gets away with all kinds of childlike behaviors, such as bursting into tears when asked to answer difficult questions. In this way, she avoids answering. Her family writes it off, as that's just the way she is. Think of the planning, the cunning, and the energy she has used over the years to maintain behaving emotionally, almost four years old, for all these decades. And, how sad to get to the White Throne Judgment and potentially have God to ask something like, *Why didn't you grow up emotionally?* Why did you manipulate all those people with guilt every time they asked you to rise above your flesh, your own desires, your own needs, and minister to them? Why didn't your soul prosper? (1 John 2)

Your emotions are part of your soul, so you should prosper emotionally. What will this 60-

something woman say to God in response to not growing up to her chronological age?

Growing Pains

Maybe it was Mattie's only sense of power in an otherwise helpless life. Perhaps every time she tries to, or tried to grow, it seemed too painful. Or, after a while it was convenient and fun to manipulate people in this way. But that doesn't make it right, since manipulation is witchcraft.

I've often thought about growing pains. In puberty and adolescence my legs and arms grew so fast that I'd wake up in the morning in pain. I'd ask my mom what was wrong with me? She'd say growing pains. For years, I thought she was just making that up. Then when I studied Medical Physiology in school, I learned that my mom is a very intelligent and wise woman; that physical pain was very real and had very real medical reasons behind why it was happening.

Emotional growing pain is real, too. We all have and need to learn certain relationship skills. For instance, sharing. It seems to me to be so much easier to learn how to share at age 2 than, at age 21. One day in a restaurant, I watched a large extended family dine, especially taking note of the way two toddlers--

, probably cousins, played with a stuffed Winnie the Pooh and a plastic truck. When a disagreement broke out, as they often do with children, the little boy was corrected and taught by his parents. But the little girl was pampered and babied by her parents. Neither child was wrong. Neither were accusing, but both were crying. I thought, sharing lesson: advantage, little boy. That little girl is going to cry a lot more before she learns sharing because. Her parents aren't helping her learn and grow.

Teaching is not always showing that 2 + 2 equals 4. Teaching is not just for the intelligence in the brain, it's also for the emotions. Teaching is showing, giving, or withholding, and sometimes disciplining.

God teaches us always, even when our heads are not in the Bible.

The little girl will have to learn sharing or continue to cry. Others will cry a lot more if she refuses to learn and no one makes her learn this joy-giving lesson. At three or four years old, this little girl is the child version of Mattie, the 60+ year old woman who is emotionally a preschooler. Being a preschooler means you haven't been to any classes or learned anything. At age 60, that's a shame.

Delayed soul, emotional growth is very much like not having chicken pox as a grade schooler, but instead having it as an adult. Chickenpox is just that, to the 10-year-old, but it causes shingles in adults, which is excruciatingly painful disease. It's much easier earlier.

CHAPTER TWELVE

GUILT & LYING

There's something demonic about evoking guilt and lying, in order to sway people to do what you want them to do. If these behaviors persist, they lay a groundwork for the *spirit of lying*. To purposefully begin lying is unwise and dangerous. A 15-year-old once asked me, *"How do you stop acting dumb?"*

What?

In order to get attention from teenage boys, she had been acting flighty and air brained for several months. Now, she did not know how to stop. Apostle Paul said, *"It's not me that worketh the sin, but the sin in me."* What he is saying is that sin, when it is allowed to persist, gets a life of its own. That's a bondage or stronghold. Acting silly has become a stronghold in her life. 10 years later, this woman still can't stop the silly behavior.

To invoke guilt purposefully is manipulative flesh work, akin to witchcraft. To lie is sin. Repetitive, compulsive lying may be the result of the bondage of sin, the *spirit of lying*. Denise, who was under the *spirit of lying*, would lie about everything, even things that didn't matter. Ask her anything and the answer would be a falsehood.

Did you go to the store, or to the library?

The answer would be a lie.

What did you buy from the store? Another lie, and so on. The *spirit* that is lying to Denise influences her greatly and the lies are not only to inconvenience or deceive that person, but they are also to indoctrinate the liar, to do something else, something worse. Compulsive and chronic liars get high in getting away with lies, so they escalate to the next level of lying, which is stealing. After stealing comes murder. If they don't have time to do it all before they die, they pass the assignment onto their children, often without being aware that they passed it on. That *spirit* or those spirits live on in family bloodlines. That's another whole book.

Demonic *spirits* try to escalate in power or increase their hold on the sinner. And unlike many professed Christians, they will work together with other *spirits* to effect horrible outcomes.

The *victim* of this oppression gives in to **relieve** the guilt that has been brought on by the manipulator. That's how the witchcraft portion of this activity works. They say things like, *If you do this or if you don't do this...* You've heard it before.

As it comes to guilt, the person to be concerned about is the person who *feels* the guilt. If the would-be victim doesn't give in, they may still feel guilty, or they may give in and then feel condemnation for giving in. Either way, weighty emotions can persist and make room for *spirit of heaviness*. This includes *apathy* and *depression*.

Depression is prevalent in today's society, and I believe that it is completely demonic. Depressed people need deliverance from the *spirit* that is oppressing them, and they need to be rescued in their emotions. They have to let go somehow of the condemnation that has come upon them. They need renewal in the Word of God, and affirmation as to who they are to God. They need to stop thinking about themselves so much. Anyone who looks too closely at themselves will surely find things wrong. For a vain person to find something wrong, it's devastating and depressing. So, the cycle continues.

Do the depressed think about themselves all day? What if Jesus had done that? I heard a minister ask once, *"What if Jesus had been too depressed to go to the cross?"* Selah.

Conversely, a people pleaser who feels that they have displeased someone may become devastated and depressed. People pleasers are the thief's targets of choice since the pleasers think of *others* all day long.

Emotional Blackmail Prayer

Strength, O, Lord, courage. Wisdom, discernment, and understanding. You, O Lord, are the Author and Finisher of all. Your Wisdom is Sovereign. Your Courage is awesome. Speak to my heart, Lord, that I may know what to do and how to do it.

Restore my soul, O Lord of David. That I may be healed of emotions that are overcharged, or emotions that overwhelm me, in the Name of Jesus. Lord, help me to be strong in the presence of enemies and thieves who want to take, trick, or deceive, by emotional ploys. Keep me, O Lord from these attacks. Strengthen me, Lord, that I might withstand, in the day of testing. I bless You, Lord, for You are the Lord of my life. In the Name of Jesus.

Amen.

CHAPTER THIRTEEN

THE SYMPATHY CHAPTER

--LEAP to the side of the offended, the hurt and the
disappointed.

Isn't it amazing that people have devised so many ways to elicit emotions and get responses and things from others? We just discussed, whining, lying and guilt in the previous chapter. Another tactic in the family of emotion-evoking thieves is sympathy.

Don't get me wrong there's a time and a place for sympathy. Jesus Himself was touched with the feelings of our infirmities. Because sympathy moves people to compassion, emotion, and action; it is a powerful motivator. It should and can provoke a lot of ministry. But misuse of it can be destructive, devastating and a time waster.

You don't automatically get sympathy when you're born. Unfortunate too, because from the warm and secure womb of your mother, you are suddenly evicted into the cold, cold world; then you get slapped. Your consolation? A blankie, a rattle and old geezers slobbering all over you.

You don't even get sympathy when you're born. You have to learn how to *make* people give you sympathy. One day as you toddle, you fall and cut your knee. Blood gushes out— you get sympathy. This is how you first learned to evoke sympathy, quite by accident, and it hurt too. Everyone is so sorry for you. Their sympathy does what? Heal you? Stop the pain? Stop the bleeding? No, it makes you feel worse. Now, besides the physical, you have learned an emotional component to this incident.

Your momma gives you a cookie if you stop crying. Sympathy, what does the cookie do, Mom? Disinfect a wound. No. Absorb the tears. No. What are the tears doing there anyway? The pain is in the knee, but the tears come out of the eyes because of the *emotions.* Now you've learned to connect these events: Fall, Pain, Tears, and Cookie.

I know Mom was just trying to distract the child from crying, but the child learned something this day. As a parent, you taught your child to cry when he falls by giving out copious amounts of sympathy, which you call, love. And, if it hurts, we get a gift. Children learn quickly that crying ***proves*** that it hurts.

Once the child finds out the benefits of crying, he will always cry, no matter if it hurts or not. As a teen or adult, he may go out into the world and do some more dumb stuff to elicit sympathy, to get gifts.

Or now that you're 15, you didn't make the cheering team. So what? Mom is so sorry, so she cooks your favorite dinner, and Dad promises to buy you a car on your birthday. What does that do? Well, that makes you go out and do something else stupid so you can come home with your lip poked out so you can get some more **stuff** from the people who *love you.*

I've decided to make a list of all the things you can buy with sympathy. ...

...The list had nothing on it.

You cannot buy anything with sympathy. You can only *steal* things with it. After getting attention and gifts when hurt or hurting, one may begin to wonder if there's a way to get this kind of response *without* **real** discomfort and pain. People may *invent* problems for others to solve, and evoke false sympathy in those who are susceptible. Doing this repeatedly will cause you to have the reputation of *pitiful*. Soon you will see yourself as the pitiful, eternal victim. Then you will *become* the perpetual victim. One day you will die unless Rapture comes first, and your report will still read, *Victim*. Is this what you want? Probably not.

Can you see yourself trying to use a sympathy ploy on God? But God..., don't even think about it. It won't work.

The transient power elicited by sympathy has your associates, friends, and family in an emotional eddy. When they are sufficiently distracted, you tell them something you want, need, or you would like to have. You're shameless. You tell them just what you want to *cheer you up*, but you're really saying is what price is required to cause you to **get over it** and go back to the way you were before the unfortunate incident. When in reality they have no responsibility to help you get over it. That's your job. The Bible says we are to possess our souls and that we are to put away works of the flesh. We are to do that *ourselves*.

The ploys may get more elaborate. The gifts may get more elaborate. When does this stop?

Brilliant. You remember when you were a kid and wanted to eat the rocks in the yard, but instead they gave you a teething ring and you forgot all about the rocks. No, you didn't.

It's the same as pointing away and saying, oh, look in aero-plane and everyone looks away while you swipe the last brownie off the plate that you knew belonged to little Shawna because she was still napping and hadn't had hers yet. That's stealing.

We are **among some thieves**, but have we *become* one of the thieves? If we exhibit these characteristics, then the answer is apparent. The devil is still using distraction as a tactic to keep you off-centered.

Now you're 29 and your husband just walked out because he's tired of your sympathy schemes. Oh, my goodness! Your mother has practically moved in with you; you're beside yourself. Your father has to pay your bills because you *suddenly* have no money. Your ex, who was a student, and never worked anyway, has **done so much <u>to</u> you** that you can't even work. What to do? What to do? Elicit sympathy, then manipulate everyone. So, for two years or forever, if you can get away with it, you talk about what that man has done to you. Stop! Exhale. Get over it. You're not the first person to have something *done* to them, and you won't be the last. Look at what Cain did to his brother. No one had sympathy for Abel. How many of us would still be expecting God to kill Cain, but He didn't?

The knee is scraped, see what you can do about it. The cheering team has already been chosen; maybe you were better at something else. Ever thought about that? Your husband is gone. Good. If he's the kind of man who would leave you, then it's good that he's gone now, instead of later. Is there really a good time to be abandoned in a relationship? No. But now that you're free, do something better, more exciting and more fulfilling with your life. You're 29.

You can't spend every day of your life wondering about everyone you've ever met or with whom you've ever had a conversation. You cannot recount each day and list the things people have *done* to you. Didn't little Bobby Loo call you a name in first grade and make you cry? How long did you carry that around? Until the sympathy ran out, right?

Did the teacher give you an F for skipping gym? Didn't you have to explain that to your parents and school counselor? No, you **earned** the F by *skipping* gym; the teacher didn't do anything to you. How long did you hate that teacher? When did you let it go? When you stopped receiving rewards for the sympathy, you emoted in those who heard *your version* of the story.

You ate an ice cream sundae last week that made your stomach hurt. Are you still carrying on about that? Are you? Are you still talking about how the restaurant on the corner makes you *feel* so you can be the center of attention and get sympathy from someone, or does your stomach really hurt? Are you asking for a Rolaids? *Then ask for Rolaids.*

If you crave sympathy or feel it is the only way you can get your way, you need deliverance. Why do we call it manipulation or control? Because Jesus should be at the center of our attention, not you, yourself. Do you see a little bit of idolatry slipping in here?

This is a difficult cycle to break and when it gets out of hand that's when it creates manipulative adults and children. Do you want results, solutions, or changes? Or do you just want the pity? Do you want to distract people into being good to you or being your friend?

Soul prosperity would attract some real good friends.

I'm not talking about all people. Some people are genuinely hurt, and sympathy is just what they need **for a season.** That's normal.

Others may become really hurt, but never even tell anyone; often these are the people pleasers.

Now the rest of you who think adopting a sympathy-craver is going to do something for you, may find yourself sorrowfully disappointed. If you are people pleaser, you are who the sympathy-craver is looking for--, to rob you of your time and *stuff*. Are you apt to say something like, *"Mary Jean is so nice. She's so sweet and everything is always happening to her. She's my friend"?*

Is she your friend or your pet project or charity case? You are the perfect target. This type of project won't earn you a raise on your job. It won't buy you a new car. It won't get you merit points for your day at the Pearly Fence. What it will get you is an emotional wear and tear that you and your body are not equipped to handle. The human body is not made to be overloaded with emotion.

And there's no way in the world you can be the emotional valve for someone else, even if you think you've mastered your own emotions. The more sympathy and attention you give the sympathy-craver, the more they want. They never get enough. Last week, their stomach hurt, this week they'll move into job harassment or brain spasms. There is no end to it unless you put an end to it. One young lady draws well-meaning people to herself several times a week. They witness to her. They offer comfort, they offer support and encouragement. She believes it's because of her attractiveness or, her "power." She was overheard saying, *"I can get anyone to pay attention to me. They stop whatever they're doing to help me."* By eliciting sympathy, she feels as though she's in control of other people, when she's not even in control of her own life.

Sound decisions are made, and battles are won with intellectual know-how, clear and level thinking, and action. None of this is possible when the emotions take over. (God may tell you to do something that seems outrageous to your mind but do it anyway. We're not talking about that.) Standing around crying is <u>not</u> an action unless God told you to stand in the gap and wail. Evoking sympathy for gifts in favor is also not an action. The emotions can override and overwork the flesh to hinder the working of the Holy Spirit, even in the saved and very Spirit-filled.

Maybe someone told you the truth and it hurt your feelings. Try not to be happy because someone had guts enough to speak the truth in love, even if the result was something you didn't like. So many of us do not have that ability, do we? Emotional growing pain really does hurt. But be thankful they cared enough to speak The truth.

What if someone took an action that offended you? Sometimes when others take action, it draws attention to our inactivity. Could that be why you're sitting around trying to get sympathy? Most want sympathy from people because of the lack of personal development. Most often these are the non-positioned in the non-purposed. Do-nothings use sympathy as a distraction from their own shortcomings or failures. Maybe you didn't get a certain job because you weren't qualified. Perhaps you didn't have a required degree. Whose fault is that? The job interviewer? No, it's yours. You don't deserve sympathy for things you chose not to do when you had the opportunity.

Let the Dead...

Misusing sympathy is when it is used as a means to divert attention from real problems. When someone dies, why are you *sorry* for them. The Bible says that the dead know nothing (Ecclesiastes 9:5), and they feel no pain. The only sympathy might be because of Judgment Day, if the person died without being saved. Don't accuse me of sounding like Doctor Spock from Star Trek. Jesus said, "...leave the dead to the dead and tend to the living. Let the dead bury their dead, (Matthew 8:22).

If you're actually thinking of the deceased, you'd be praying that they accepted Jesus Christ, and rejoicing that they now passed on, having finished their course. If you had really cared, you would have been witnessing to them while they were alive, encouraging them to present their bodies a living sacrifice, not a half dead, or deceased sacrifice. Praise God for the homegoing. Yes, goodbyes can be tearful, but if they are with God and why are you still crying? Are those tears of joy? They are with God and not with you.

The person's death is not really about you, it's between the deceased and God. None us may ever know what deals anyone has made with God.

Let the Living

Scriptures say to be absent from the body is to be present with the Lord, which is the same as being out of the flesh and into the *Spirit*. Millions of people every day seek to be in the **presence** of God. Are you sorry for the millions of believers and worshippers in the world seeking the face of God? Of course not. Why not? Because they're only worshipping. They're coming back.

They really aren't. If they've been in the presence of God when they come back, **they won't be the same ever again.** No one is ever the same after having been in the presence of God. If you really worship every time you go into the presence of God, you change from Glory to Glory. So let the living seek the Lord while they can.

Let the dead who have earned their rewards enjoy their rewards.

Excessive Sympathy Only Distracts

No solution can be achieved with an excited, overactive, depressed, or distracted mind. One must stay centered and objective every day, all day. Regarding the Fruit of the Spirit, having peace is what New Agers call being "centered." But they stole that from the Church. Truly, what does the world know about peace?

Showing compassion and care to those in distress or discomfort is godly, but sympathy should not be for the purpose of earning people gifts and rewards. Over-givers have sympathy, (people pleasers), or over-receivers of sympathy (thieves) have taken their eyes off the correct prize. Sympathy cravers have their eyes on temporal and man-made prizes.

Looking unto Jesus, the author and finisher of our faith, who for the joy that was set before him endured the cross, despising the shame. And it is set. At the right hand of the throne of God, (Hebrews 12:2).

It's Not Love

Sympathy-abuse is a devious trick in a devilish trap. Watch for it. Instead of sympathy, LEAP to the side of the offended, hurt, disappointed.

L-Love them.

E- Exhort them. Edify them.

A- Assist them as they grieve, but don't let them stay there.

P- Pray for them. And with them, have patience with them as they go through disappointment.

Chronic sympathy is debilitating and crippling. An infant's father was tragically killed. The resulting sympathy from a bevy of uncles and aunts allowed the child to do whatever she liked, whenever she liked. No rules, no bedtime, candy all the time, or gifts every time they saw the child-- because she had no father. Since the child, unfortunately, and suddenly has no father, that child needs *more* discipline, more guidelines, more self-control, et cetera, so when the day comes, if she finds herself really alone, there will be someone to lean on --herself and Jesus Christ. But self-reliance should not be relinquished for reliance on another human being, food, or worldly gifts. When lessons in life should be taught, don't give rewards when they are not learned. Because receiving rewards constantly makes the student think he's doing well, or that everything is alright.

No one can love, support, or treat you as well as Jesus. And after Jesus, **you** are next in line to love yourself and treat yourself well. The orphan child should be taught the love of Christ and self-love immediately and *without ceasing,* instead of just being showered with sympathy and gifts. Sympathy gifts teach the child to rely on *people and things* rather than Jesus.

Have the mind of Christ give gifts out of love,

care, relationship and not out of sympathy.

THE SYMPATHY PRAYER

Dear Heavenly Father, Wonderful is Your Name. The Earth, O Lord is filled with Your Mercy. Thank You, Lord, for Mercy and Grace, for divine favor. Thank You, Lord, for Your unchanging ways. Thank You for not wandering wavering when it concerns us. Thank You, Lord, for being Lord of our souls.

We come to You today in the Name of Jesus to ask that our Wisdom will increase, and our discernment heightened, that our minds will be clear, that our thinking will be more like Jesus. That the mind that is in us, will be like the mind that is also in Christ Jesus. We ask Lord, that You will keep us from those who use sympathy as a form of blackmail. To coax or trick us into doing things that we might not otherwise do.

We repent, Lord, for the times we have used sympathy either ignorance or outright deceit, to achieve our own goals. We know that we have a God who is touched with the feelings of our infirmities. But we know You are the Mighty God who cannot be tricked. Like You, we also do not want to be tricked by the enemy, the Thief. We bless You today, Lord, for delivering us from sympathy abuse, in the Name of Jesus, Amen.

CHAPTER FOURTEEN

BUT IT'S FAMILY

& SUCCESS BREEDS RELATIVES

The Bible is all about families, generations, and relationships. Families should stick together. Chances are good that you've grown up in a family where *family* is stressed, looking out for one another, taught modeled and expected. You've been instructed that blood is thicker than water.

Better Than

There have probably been times, as a child, that you've had to share or give something to another just because they were your brother or sister, but it may have conflicted with your own desires as an adult. If your brother or sister asked something of you that you felt is not quite right or something you did not want to do, you may have done it anyway with your parents' voice echoing in your head, *"We're family."*

If you have doubts about the way you were being treated by your family, especially concerning the things that you're asking of you pose and answer these questions, would I accept this treatment from or do this for a stranger? Would you accept this type of behavior from your neighbor across the street? Would I do this for my neighbor? Would I do it for a stranger? Be objective. If the answer is no, then why accept it from your family?

Your family should treat you **better than** not worse than they would treat strangers. Your families should treat you **better than** your boss or coworkers at the office, and you expect them to treat you **better than** an acquaintance, because you treat them **better than** all of those other people in your life. And because you've heard, *"We're family,"* all your life, that really means something to you. That's why you make a sacrifice to go out of your way to do things for your relatives. But that's also why family betrayals are so devastating.

If someone cuts you off on the freeway, you may become offended, angered, or disappointed in them, and their driving, but you usually get over it quickly. But people you live with, are related to and have seen all of your life have your trust. You did not really trust the driver on the freeway. You may have hoped and prayed that they would be a diligent driver, but you have invested no real time or interest in them, but your investment in your family member, who may have subsequently betrayed you, disappointed you or let you down with *substantial*.

Who Are *These* People?

A friend loveth at all times, and a brother is born for adversity, (Proverbs 17:17).

Many things are worked out in us by fellowship. Some things are brought out in us by our relatives. Sometimes God gives us relationships with people who have character and behavior similar to ours, and oftentimes we are related to them. Jesus said, **For whosoever shall do the will of God the same is my brother and my sister and mother,** (Mark 3:35).

Sometimes the family can suddenly and unexpectedly *grow*. I'm not talking about sudden births, instead, that thing that happens when a little success or notoriety becomes associated with a name. What if that happened to Jesus as His fame went out through the land? I wonder if He had cousins to just show up out of nowhere. John the Baptist was his cousin, and he had natural, brothers and sisters. But I wonder how many people just came to Him for favors. Just as the mayor gets requests to fix traffic or parking tickets? As the person working behind whatever counter in a retail establishment gets requests from friends, relatives, or even bold strangers for discounts, I wonder how many people slipped up to Jesus and asked for a *touch, or a real quick* blessing? How many were trying to avoid protocols, so they didn't have to go through the regular channels--, you know, the **Multitude**?

Now that you're a business owner or promoted to the corner office with a firm you've been with for 12 years, how many new *cousins* do you have who are so proud of you and knew you *when*? And how many of them are asking for favors such as money or to borrow your new sports car, free professional advice. How are you handling yourself? Chances are good that if you've gotten this far in your career and profession, then you know how to handle moochers, new fifth cousins, and twice removed relatives.

Give, but don't be taken advantage of, the Word says to be wise, seek and use Wisdom.

CHAPTER FIFTEEN

FEAR IS A THIEF

Fear is worrying about losing something you *think* you own.

Fear can be devastating. You need courage to overcome that fear, courage to be more than the devil's door mat. As long as you're in fear, you are not operating in Bible principles and overcoming. When bound by fear, you're really defeated. You can't fight back if you're tied up; that's what **bound** is. Sometimes fear can be so intense that a person could be bound and defeated by the fear; sometimes just being bound is enough. In order for the devil to steal from you, you must first bind you, just as a strongman is first bound and then spoiled, (Mark 3:27). That's a strategy we must learn to *reverse* so it does not get used on us, but instead we use it on the enemy.

Here's a practical test:

1.   What is your definition of fear?

My definition of fears the absence of peace, the absence of God-knowledge, the absence of the Comforter, the presence of worry.

> And I will pray the father, and he shall give you another comforter that he may abide with you forever, (John 14:16).

2. **Of what are you afraid?**
3. **Why?**
4. **Of whom are you afraid?**
5. **Why?**
6. **Are your above-listed fears of known or unknown things?**
7. **Are they fears of something you've experienced personally**, or something that someone--, a parent, a sibling or a friend has told you, or warned you of? Or something you read about or saw on TV?
8. Do you want to get over those fears? Really?
9. Do you like discussing your fears and phobias?

If you *enjoy* discussing your fears, phobias, and horrible experiences, then you're not ready to let them go. If you use fears and phobias to get attention or sympathy, you are using demonic activity for personal, temporal, and foolish gain. You're also bringing glory and attention to Satan's Kingdom.

All fears culminate into the fear of death. Death of what? Usually the death of whatever you fear you may lose.

> For the thing which I greatly feared is come upon me

and that which I am afraid of is come unto me, (Job 3:25).

It could be the death or demise of relationships, job successes, attention, health, or beauty, to name a few. Even the fear of gaining weight preoccupies the minds of millions. Whatever the fear or phobia, no matter how slight, it is in the opening of the door for the *spirit of fear*.

Should the saved, born-again man be afraid? No; for God has not given us a *spirit of fear*, but one of love and power, and of a sound mind, (2 Timothy, 1:7). Should the Spirit-filled man be afraid? No, for God has not given us the *spirit of fear*, but one of love, power, and a sound of mind. Was fear in the Garden of Eden? No.

Did God put a *spirit of fear* In Adam? No. If he had, Adam and Eve would never have interacted with the Serpent; they wouldn't have gone near it. How many folks do you know who are afraid of snakes? Too many folks. When the Serpent crawled into the Garden of Eden, Adam and Eve would have run if they had had the *spirit of fear.* But they stayed there and were disobedient and duped.

Of what was Jesus afraid? I don't believe that Jesus was ever afraid, but in the Garden of Gethsemane He was at a sensitive and critical place that was never again recorded in His experiences while here on Earth. It was the only time He called God, *ABBA*, which translated means, *Daddy*. The translators of the Bible (KJV), were very much slanted to formal English, and Jesus spoke of God as Father or Lord through the New Testament, except on this one occasion. Jesus needed God as Daddy at this time because of the difficulty with the upcoming events. The Scripture reads that we have not received the *spirit of fear,* but the *spirit of adoption*, and therefore we cry, ABBA, (Romans 8:15).

Jesus had asked mere men to watch Him pray for Him as He struggled with this final thing to finish the work. They had ascended to the Garden of Gethsemane, which is itself a feat. The mountain is quite steep. Holy Land tourists walk it, but they stop to rest along the way. I walked it, alongside a 20-year-old who did not have enough stamina to make the climb without a break. Jesus was 33 years old then and being dirt, grass, or stones at that time, it was probably more difficult to scale to the top. Where most of us, including the 20-year-old would be complaining about the climb. Jesus had so much more ahead of Him.

Jesus was in Gethsemane talking to God about the next things that were to happen. He knows He's to be betrayed by Judas, then turned over to the Romans. He knows about the trials, and the crucifixion. But the worst thing of all was knowing that God would have to turn His back on Him as He carried **our** sin to the Cross.

Any of us might be still complaining about how tired we are. We'd complain that it's dark, we can't see very clearly, or we talk about the mosquitoes or any other biting bugs that come around, especially at night when a person is sweating.

How many of us could get past the betrayal by Judas? Not many of us. Judas, a person we've handpicked, and ministered to, and with for 3 1/2 years, who is right at that time selling us out for chump change--, the cost of a slave? I have a feeling that most of us would still be mad at Judas, having vengeance in our hearts as the Romans flogged, then crucified Jesus.

The average human would still be in Hell, planning revenge on Judas and having plans to get the rest of the money back that Judas had stolen from the treasury.

But thankfully Jesus was not carnal as He struggled with the assignment. He comes up twice to see if His intercessors are doing their job. They sleep.

The same Jesus who was asleep as a storm came, while they were in the boat going to the other side but was awakened with only a call and a cry. Jesus did not turn over and go back to sleep. This same Jesus needs them, but they sleep while He's going through the most horrific night of His ministry here on Earth. This was much more gruesome than being tempted of the devil after 40 days and nights of fasting and consecration, after submersion by John the Baptist.

He calls out to God as Daddy as a hurt, lonely, sad child who needs his parent. But Jesus did not carry the *spirit of fear* in Him. He was filled, the Bible says, with Grace and Wisdom and Truth, so there was no room for anything that was not like God.

From where does the *spirit of fear* come? The devil. After the first sin. Adam and Eve then decided to hide themselves from God after they had disobeyed Him. Now they **have *fear***. How ironic.

Interesting how *fear* is grouped in the same verse with Love, Power, and a Sound Mind. It takes all of that: Love, Power, and a Sound Mind to overcome the *spirit of fear*. So don't think that if you don't overcome fear right away that is hopeless, or something is wrong with you.

Why all this talk about *fear*? So, you can understand more about yourself and why you allow things to happen **_to_** you and around you instead of taking control. It's all about becoming the person you're supposed to be, to become a better you, so you can encourage yourself and witness to, and minister to others.

What is the hope that is set before you? What is the joy that is set before you? What is the promise that God is whispered into your spirit? What is the promise that burns in your soul? Don't let **fear** block your next blessing. Don't let the Thief called Fear, rob you.

Phobias

A persistent, irrational fear of, and desire to avoid a particular object or situation, is a *phobia*. Minor phobias do not impair daily life; major ones do. Intense phobias cause anxiety and can lead to panic attack.

> For we have not received the *spirit of bondage* again to fear. But you have received the *spirit of adoption*. Whereby we cry, ABBA, Father, (Romans 8:15).

These Scriptures are listed for you at edification. When fear comes upon you, say the Scriptures that apply to your situation out loud. Say them often until they get in your spirit, then celebrate how the Lord has delivered you from the fears that plague you.

Anxiety

Be careful for nothing but in everything by prayer and supplication with Thanksgiving. Let your request be made known unto God, (Philippians 4:6).

For the Lord shall be thy confidence, and she'll keep thy foot from being taken. Withhold not good from them to whom it is due when it is in their power of blind hand to do it, (Proverbs 3:25-26).

Heights & Flying

Have I not commanded? They be strong and of good courage. Be not afraid. Neither be thou dismayed for the Lord thy God is with thee. Whithersoever thou goest, (Joshua 1:9).

Where shall I go from thy spirit? For whither shall I flee from thy presence if I send up into the heavens? Thou art there. If I make my bed in hell, behold thou art there. If I take the wings of the morning and dwell in the uttermost parts of the Sea, (Psalms 139:7-8)

For he shall give his angels charge over the to keep the oil five ways, (Psalm 91:11).

Animals & Monsters

At destruction and famine. Thou shalt laugh. Neither shalt thou be afraid of the beast of the earth, (Job 5:22).

God has given us dominion over the beasts of the Earth. Fowls of the air, and the fish of the sea. How can we exercise Dominion if we have *fear*? Fear persists if we think on it. We should immediately cast out fearful things, people, places, and situations that could only potentially harm us. Those with a vivid imagination should limit fright and things that scare them.

Casting down imaginations and every high thing that exalts if itself against the knowledge of God and bringing it to captivity, every thought to the obedience of Christ, (2 Corinthians 10:5).

Water, Floods & Swimming

Remember that God is with us always, (Psalms 139:9-11).

And there arose a great storm of wind, and the waves beat the ship so that it was now full. And he was in the Hydra part of the ship, asleep on a pillow. And they awake him and say unto him, master cares, though not that we perish, and he arose and rebuked the wind and said into the sea, peace be still, and the wind seized. And there was a great calm, (Mark 4:37- 39).

Thunderstorms

Say to the storm peace be still, (Mar 4:39).

Death

Yea, though walk through the valley of the shadow of death, I will fear no evil. (Psalms 23:4).

Oh, death. Where's thy staying? O grave, where is thy victory? The sting of death is sin. And the strength of sin is the law, (1 Corinthians 15:55-56).

To be absent from the body is to be present with the Lord, (2 Corinthians 5:8).

Claustrophobia: Elevators, Closets, Darkness

The Lord is my light and my salvation. Whom shall I fear? The Lord is the strength of my life. Of whom shall I be afraid? (Psalms 27:1).

He that dwelleth in the secret place of the most high, shall abide under the shadow of the Almighty, (Psalms 91:1).

Thou shall not be afraid of the terror by night, nor for the arrow that flieth by day, (Psalms 91:5).

If I say, surely the darkness shall cover me, even the night. Shelby light about me? Yeah, the darkness height. If not from the but the night shineth as the day. The darkness and the light are both alike to thee, (Psalms 139:12).

Your Enemies

And command thou the people saying you are to pass through the coast of your brethren, the children of Esau, which dwell in sear, and they shall be afraid of you. Take a good heat unto yourselves, therefore, (Deut 24).

The Lord is my light and my salvation. Whom shall I fear? The Lord is the strength of my life. Of whom shall I be afraid? (Psalms 27:1).

Be not afraid of their faces, for I'm with the to deliver these sayeth the Lord. (Jeremiah 1:8).

Fear of Being Alone

Fear not, for I am with thee, (Isaiah 43:5).

I will never leave the nor forsake thee, (Hebrews 13-5).

Remember Jehovah Shammah, the God who is always with you.

Nightmares & Monsters

He gave it to his beloved sleep, (Psalms 127:2).

When thou list down, thou shalt not be afraid. Yeah, thou shalt lie down and die. Sleep shall be sweet, (Proverbs 3:24).

Not be afraid for the terror by night, nor for the arrow

that flies by day, nor for the pestilence that block if and

darkness, (Psalms 91:5-6).

Casting down imagination, (2 Corinthians 10:5).

Lies & Persecution

Bless it are ye, when men shall revile you and persecute you, and shall say all manner of evil against you falsely. For my sake, (Matthew 5:11).

No weapon that is formed against the shall prosper, and every tongue that shall rise against the in judgment thou shalt condemn. This is the heritage of the servants of the

Lord, and their righteousness is of me safe. The Lord
(Isaiah 54:17).

Night Fears

When thou lies down, thou shalt not be afraid, but thou shalt lie down, and I sleep. Shall be sweet, (Proverbs 3:24).

As an adult, I've lived alone many years through college and other times as well. There have been evenings when retiring for bed I would hear and sense strange noises. Instead of struggling with sleep. I would get up and walk through my house. Blessing it. I would pray real prayers of protection over myself and my dwelling. By my words, I give God's angels charge over me to keep me in all my ways. With my voice, I say, *"The Lord is my helper. I shall not fear what man can do,"* (Hebrews 13:6). Opening my mouth and using my breath, I verbally remind myself and every Angel, good or bad, that God is Omnipotent, Sovereign and able to keep me. I praise God that no harm shall come nigh me, or my dwelling place. I thank Him for giving *rest* to his beloved. That's me.

Then I go to sleep.

After a while, depending on your faith, you will not hear or sense noises. Instead, you will have perfect peace. Then you can sleep at night.

He shall not be afraid of evil tidings. His heart is fixed, trusting in the Lord. His heart is established, and he shall not be afraid until he see his desires upon his enemies, (Psalms 112:7-8).

No Fear In Love

There's No Fear in love, but perfect love casts without fear because fear hath torment he that feareth is not me. Perfect in love, (1 John 4:18).

You fear the unknown because you don't love it.

You can't love it because you don't know it.

Perfect love does not fear what the husband or the wife is doing where they are, or with whom. Perfect love lifts up and doesn't tear down. Perfect love keeps no account of wrongs done. Perfect love covers a multitude of sin and forgives. Jesus is our perfect love, and He calls us to love one another perfectly as well--, not just in romantic relationships, but to all the Saints of God as well, but also when we love perfectly, when we love Jesus perfectly and also love one another. Fear is not part of our thought life, our vocabulary, and it does not torment us. How is your **real** love life? If you were living in fear? Then your *love life* needs work.

Aliens

Quench the violence of fire. Escape the edge of the sword of the weakness. Were made strong, waxed valiant in flight, turned to flight. The armies of the aliens (Heb 11:34)

Martians? UFOs? No, that's not what the Bible is talking about. Aliens are folk that don't belong in the places, the spaces, the faces of stuff God is giving you; these things are thieves. If you're afraid of them, you may not fight. And if you don't fight, you can't be victorious.

Courage

Courage is the quality of character which shows itself in facing danger bravely or enacting despite fear or lack of confidence.

Be strong enough. Good courage, fear not, nor be afraid of them. For the Lord thy God he is that Duff. Go with me. He will not fail thee, nor forsake thee, (Deut 31:18).

Be strong and of good courage, (Deuteronomy 31:6).

Have not I commanded thee be strong enough? Good courage. Be not afraid. Neither be thou dismayed for the Lord thy God is with thee. Whithersoever thou goest, Joshua 19. Be of good courage. He shall strengthen your heart, all ye that hope in the Lord, (Psalm 31:24).

The House of Fear

You need courage to be who you are and to say no to the thieves. All of them, especially the thief called *fear*. If you were to look in the House of Fear. If there's a such a place, you'd find more things that belong to God's people than in any other place. Most of the things taken from God's people are not released to God's people is because of *fear*.

In this hypothetical space, you find few physical weapons, but instead spiritual weapons that especially torment, the mind, imagination, thoughts and ideas. You find misinformation, misconception, noises and mind games. Sometimes that torment is in the form of thought. Sometimes those thoughts are personified and show up on the faces of friends or even family members. You need to be aware to see tricks that people who are being used by the devil, use to deceive you. People pleaser, you need courage to speak up; say, "No!" to being duped, "*niced*," or coerced into things that you know better than to do.

The lion needed courage in the Wizard of Oz. That's ironic. How can he, by definition, be a lion if he needs courage? You're ironic. How can you be all that God says that you *are* when you're *not*. I'm ironic for the same reason. But by faith through prophecy, the Word, by reflecting and mirroring by loved ones and relations, we come to know who we are, then we **become** who we are, in Him.

Have you ever noticed everything that was lacking in the Wizard of Oz was due to spiritual oppression or ignorance? Courage, heart, mind, and home. Note that fear took the travelers into dark and dangerous places and kept them there. **You've** got to activate what's already in you by the power of faith. God has not given you fear--, instead He has given you courage. You are a mighty man of valor; more than a conqueror.

If you don't have courage to deal with the unseen things, how will you deal with the faces of the *people* who are looking at you tomorrow at the office? How will you have courage to say, "No!" to the thieves that you may find yourself among if you don't expel the *spirit of fear*? If you're still bound when the fight begins, you cannot expect to win. Being free to fight and knowing that you are free to fight adds to courage and we all need courage always.

FEAR & COURAGE PRAYER

In Your Word, Lord, You said whatsoever we bind on Earth shall be bound in Heaven, and whatsoever we loose on Earth shall be loosed in Heaven, (Matthew 18:18).

We come to You today, Mighty God, in the Name of Jesus, binding the *spirit of fear* and casting it out. You have not given us a *spirit of fear,* but of love, power, and a sound mind. We receive the Spirit You have given us, Lord. We loose the *spirit of love* and power and a sound mind, and claim the **spirit of adoption** so that we can call you, Abba, Father. We claim defeat to the work of the enemy in our life. We ask you, Lord, for boldness and courage, to speak up and speak out, not only for our preservation, but to the edification of the Saints and to the Glory of Your Name.

Thank You, Lord, that we can cast down imaginations, walk victoriously and overcome any fear, phobia, or anxiety that the enemy has set as a trap or as a stumbling block before us. Thank You, Lord, for giving Your angels charge over us to keep us in all our ways. Thank You that no harm shall come to us and that no harm shall come to our homes. Thank You for keeping us safe and our daily travels and being our God and Helper, in the Name of Jesus.

Amen.

Why Didn't You Do It?

Who didn't go,

didn't try,

didn't know,

didn't fly,

because of fear?

Who didn't rest,

didn't bless,

didn't test,

because of fear?

Some didn't give,

didn't live,

because of fear.

What dismay to find

that the shadow you saw that.

Provoked the fear, was only

a shadow because Light

was near!

Go! Try! Know! Fly!

Rest! Bless! Test! Live!

Conquer fear; The Light is Near.

Dr. Marlene Miles \, c, 2000

Once you realize that you don't own *anything,*

including your life, once you realize that you're only called to stewardship, you will NEVER fear again!

CHAPTER SIXTEEN

HEALTH THIEVES

---Emotions can abuse an individual's health.

Just as a doormat picks up dirt off the feet and shoes that trample it, the soul picks up, hurts, disappointments, betrayals, and deceit from those who tread over it. Emotions, especially the soul of a people pleaser--, all those words that the people pleaser left unsaid in hopes of maintaining harmony may cause soul hurts. Things held back in hopes that *this* time the insensitive or over-aggressive person would see the error of their ways and *change*. All that fear, which kept a person closed up, bound up and wound up, can cause devastation to the health. As the abused or battered wife might keep things bottled up thinking, *This time I will love him more even more than last time. This time I will treat them as Jesus would.* Hoping for a sudden transformation and hoping to draw him to the loving kindness of Jesus as it manifests through that hopeful people pleaser.

Good morning, People Pleaser; *wake up.*

Now the Peacemaker is different in this situation; the Peacemaker has been **sent**, the peacemaker has been anointed and filled to do this difficult job, even **among some thieves**. The Peacemaker has grace sufficient to take care of the spiritual business and not be adversely affected. If God has graced you and appointed you to handle a difficult person or situation, and you do what He tells you, how He tells you, then the Health Thief cannot steal from you. But those nice people, the people pleasers, who take it upon themselves, really do *take it upon themselves*.

Dogs & Swine

Give not that which is holy into the dogs, neither cast your pearls before swine Lest they trample them under their feet and turn again and rend you, (Matthew 7:16).

The Thief has many faces. The Word makes this very simple. We don't even need discernment to avoid this mistake, only sense. In the above Scripture, we only need the *sense of hearing*; we can tell that as a dog by its bark. In the case of the pig, we only need the *sense of smell*. The stench of a pigsty can clue us that a pig is nearby. Further, the verse tells us that these two ungrateful types, the pig and the dog, will trample that which is valuable under their feet, not using it wisely or giving it any worth. *And if that's not enough, then they will turn on you* and attempt to tear you to bits.

You've met those types of people who are ungrateful tramplers, who will turn on you for their wants and convenience. I've talked about them in preceding chapters, and now we've come to the place where we discuss what the dirt of their trampling can do to your body. What the soil of their selfishness, and the dirt of their deceit can grow in you, in a real sense. It may not be evident or even manifest right away, but if the *tread marks* are not removed, the stains remain indelible and permanent. If hurt emotions are not released or dealt with, they have the ability to cause devastation in the human body.

I have often believed that the cause of many diseases is emotional. It is as much what we go through as our perception of what happened to us in those situations that leave their *marks* on us. Diseases and infirmities, disorders and sickness, diseases are the results of emotional wear and tear on the soul. These diseases manifest in the body at the place of weakness or generational predisposition.

Have you ever wondered why a person can smoke all their lives, but their lungs remain cancer or emphysema-free? Yet a nonsmoker may have problems with their lungs even early in life?

Generational predisposition. Some families have very strong lungs, while other families may have very strong hearts, but their lungs may not be as strong, for example.

God wants all of us to be very strong and in health in every organ system in our body, but because of genetics which passes on family information at the cellular level, some families appear to be weak or strong in certain organs or systems of the body because of generational curses. Some families appear spiritually weaker in certain parts of their bodies.

This is why it is critical that families reveal their histories to their children, doctors say so for medical reasons. But I say so for *spiritual reasons*. How will your child or grandchild know what to pray for if they don't know what's wrong with Grandma, or what Grandpa died of?

Al, a 45-year-old, churchgoing businessman, does not know what his natural father, who raised him from birth, died of. When asked, he states that his father *just got a cold and died*. I pressed to see if Al was avoiding the answer, but he really didn't know. What about his own life? How will he know what to avoid if it were food related? How would he know what to avoid if it were lifestyle related? How would he know what to avoid if it were medical or pharmaceutical? How we know how to pray or if he needs to tear down strongholds or if it's a generational curse? How we know how to fight, how to win, and how to live? He won't. And while living under this deception that a *cold* caused the demise of his father, he may be overtaken by something else. As faith comes by hearing, this man may really believe that a cold took his daddy out, and so believing he may also succumb to a common cold.

Inside Out

Emotional wear and tear is the result of the thief operating at the second level. The first level was the stealing of Peace, Joy, Time, or something emotionally or tangibly important or valuable from you. The Thief doesn't stop there. He attacks at a second level based on your *reactions* to the theft. Then he becomes the Health Thief.

Too many only become aware of this devastation at *bodily manifestation*.

So, the devil can try to hurt your body, for example, in a car accident, that's from the outside, in. Or you may try to cause you to hurt yourself through overactive emotions from the inside, out. Emotional or soul affliction. If a person is obsessed, or over personalizes everyday events or is easily vexed or devastated, the attacks work from the inside, out.

Sometimes it seems people's experiences express literally in their bodily manifestations. An elderly, sickly woman whose children ask her for money all the time continues to give and give in spite of her own needs. Sacrifice is beautiful; Jesus did it, but He also knew when to pull away from the crowds to be alone. This woman doesn't. Her kids are robbing her blind. The manifestation is her eyesight; she has been diagnosed as legally blind.

The Sound Mind

In order to get past this stuff, you have been through, you will need the following: Love, Power, and a Sound Mind. You will need Love because the works of the flesh such as hatred, jealousy, unforgiveness and bitterness breed illness in the body. **Un**forgiveness, it is said, leads to chronic neck pain, stiff neck. Unresolved unforgiveness leads to the root of bitterness, which shows up as an attack on the kidneys. Love overcomes unforgiveness and bitterness.

You need Power. You need Power to bring your own flesh under subjection and resist the devil that he so that he will flee from you. You will need what the world calls willpower. You can't do the things that the world commonly does; you cannot do everything that your unsaved neighbor is doing and expect God to bless you. You need to set your will **not** to do worldly things. You are called to holiness, and in order to live in holiness, you must first *decide* that you **will** live in holiness and then have Power to resist temptation. You are called to forgiveness. Forgiving a hurt, takes faith and it takes power. Forgiveness also heals, and it will heal you.

You need a Sound Mind so you can *think on these things*, (Philippians 4:8), instead of the things that bring on fears and negative emotions. The devil will give you plenty to think about, and plenty that you need to resist. Just because you have a thought doesn't mean it came from God. Just because you have a thought doesn't mean you are to dwell on it. Many of your thoughts or a result of what *you* see, and what *you* hear. By guarding your heart with all diligence, (Proverbs 4:23), you guard your Sound Mind. You make the final choice daily about holiness. You make the final decision daily about what you're going to watch on television, what music you will listen to, what people you will listen to and what books and magazines you will read. Those decisions then open or close the gates for the devil to work through. So, if you are tired of having nightmares, you may want to stop watching horror movies or reading certain kinds of books. If you go to a restaurant that serves meat, the waiter will expect that meat is what you came for. If you open your eyes and ears to certain things, God will *allow* you to receive those things. What you *allow* God allows, but what you **bind** God will also bind, (Matthew 18:18).

When studying Human Pathology, I was amazed that every week several medical students, not always the same ones, would start to imagine that they were exhibiting the symptoms of whatever horrible human disease of the flesh we were studying. If the disease of the week was skin-related, many students would not only check their bodies for sores, lesions, eruptions, or nevi. They sat around talking about it among themselves. The fear was planted individually, then the *Fearful's* encouraged one another in their worry.

As far as I know, no one in particular Pathology class, actually contracted any of these dread diseases, but it's become apparent that they didn't have the sound mind that Paul wrote Timothy about. It was unfortunate that they didn't know that neither the author of the textbook nor the worldly instructor of the class were prophets of God and able to speak things into their lives. The manifestations of disease did not come to any of these students that year, because their faith to create the negative, which is fear, was not developed well enough to bring it to pass during that Course.

But what seeds were planted in the minds of those would-be healers. Some of these are now **Dr. Fearful's,** who may be practicing medicine in your town. Perhaps this is why some doctors are so dramatic when they actually do find the manifestation of disease in patients. Perhaps they are expressing their own fears. They give the horrible life changing and life-threatening reports. Often these reports are devoid of hope. That's why <u>you</u> need a relationship with God. Acknowledge Him to know who you should allow to diagnose and speak into ***your*** life.

A Non-Believer will speak non-believing things in non-believing ways.

If you must have a non-believer as a doctor, diagnose you (for example), one of you should be balanced with Wisdom and the power of the Holy Spirit. Don't rely on the doctor's *faith*. <u>It must be you.</u>

O, My Soul!

Doctors say that when an emotional attack comes to the body, it depresses the immune system. When the immune system is weak, it's when the devil will want to wage an Inside-Out attack. Every time that incident is rehearsed or remembered, the ability of the immune system to protect the body is lessened. Whatever body part or organ you maybe weekend may suffer, if attacked. Even if the incident that hurt, disappointed, or frightened you happened 20 years ago, when you remember it, it is as though you are right there living it again.

You need a Sound Mind to stop thinking on the hurts of your past, no matter how little or big they are. No matter what someone dared or what you think they did to you, thinking on it hurts you. You need a Sound Mind to stop using the offenses or experiences of the past to make another look bad or draw attention to yourself.

Remember, you need love in order to forgive.

That's why we have a Praise Report. That's why we give our testimony. The testimony has two parts. Part One is what happened to us or what the devil tried to cause to happen to us. And Part 2 is how God brought us through. Nowhere in the Bible does it say that we shall overcome by whining, rehearsing wrongs done to us, or giving testimony about what the devil has done to us. No, it says just the opposite. We testify to the goodness of God, and if God has brought us through, we dwell on His Mercy, Grace, and Favor toward us. And there are other benefits to the praise report.

- It blesses those who hear it.
- It builds our own faith and blesses us.
- It blesses God!

So, talk about what the Lord has done for you. ***They overcame by the blood of the Lamb and the Word of their testimony.*** Overcome by how much Word is in your testimony. Talk about the goodness of the Lord!

The world is not that way. Many would rather talk about the illness than how they received a cure. Many would rather talk about the disease rather than their recovery from that disease. Many talk about the horrors or fear of the surgery rather than the outcome, or that they're not able to walk, for instance, because of their successful knee replacement surgery. You've heard many women talk about the negative effects of childbirth. That's not us. That should not be the church.

Emotional hurts really do hurt, but it's up to us to stop them from damaging *our minds and our bodies*. It's up to us not to allow past offenses or betrayals to get down into our soul and spirit, because if they get into your flesh and take root, they will be passed on *generationally*. Don't let a negative experience you had five years ago cause your child or grandchild to suffer by rehearsing it in your family life. Don't hold it in, until it makes you physically sick, causing someone to have to take care of you in your illness. By encoding the negative response forever into your genes, into your generations. Could it be that the family with weak hearts, in the natural was the family that didn't have *heart* in the spiritual? They were fearful, fearful, fearful. Probably.

If that's the case, that proves that the cause and solution to every physical problem is *spiritual*.

Don't allow your child to see what the devil can do as if you don't even know God or have the power of forgiveness and Love.

Give a testimony, not a complaint.

It's true, hurts really do hurt. But with the Lord, you can bear it, cast it out, overcome it, and forgive those who hurt you. Jesus did; and He is our Supermodel.

They overcame by the blood of the lamb and by the word of their testimony. (Revelations 12:11).

PRAYER AGAINST HEALTH THIEVES

Dear Heavenly Father, my healer, Jehovah, Rapha, in the Name of Jesus, I come to You for help in time of healing for my body and emotions. You restore my soul. You are the Great Physician. Help me, Lord, to avoid being taken advantage of by people, be they Thieves or just confused folks.

You are the Lord of my life. Your Joy is my strength. Help me to please You, Lord in my decisions and actions. Keep me, Lord, so I don't harbor hurt, anger or resentment of past pain in my heart or in my body. Even diseases that have not manifested in my body, but the devil may have begun the Inside-Out attack on me, I cut off at the root, in Jesus Name.

Help me, Lord to let it go, to release it from my body. Help me to forgive, to release people who've hurt me. Help me to forgive, Lord even as You forgive me.

Keep my mind in perfect peace. Keep my body in perfect health, to Your Glory. In the Name of Jesus, I know You are well able to give me divine help and I receive it today, in the Name of Jesus, to the Glory of God and the Kingdom of Heaven. Amen.

Count it all Joy. Don't worry. Be Healthy.

If nothing ever happened to you, you'd have no complaints. If you never had a complaint, you'd never call on God.

If God never bought you through, you'd have no testimony. If you had no testimony, you'd have no ministry.

No ministry means no purpose.

Whatever you're going through, I have been through count it all Joy.

CHAPTER SEVENTEEN

LIFE THIEVES

That would make an interesting story, wouldn't it? The story of the successful professional turn bad. Perhaps he's been exposed as a wife beater or caught as an adulterer or using drugs. That would make an incredible story, an interesting newspaper or magazine article, a bestselling book, and a dynamite movie. So, what if it's someone else's real life? A story like this could set you on top. It could get you noticed. It could get you just what you need to make your mark in the world. Whether in journalism, politics, law, or even show business. You always wanted your own talk show. This could be your chance.

Someone Else's *Real* Life

After all that hard work, a thief comes along, stepping on the ones who've done all the work, made the sacrifices to propel him or herself up to the next level. All that work was foundation and steppingstones for the generations that were to proceed from the loins of that hard-working individual. Yet it has been stolen not only from that individual, but from his children.

Also, his good name has been stolen, along with inheritance status, title or respect by the Life thieves.

Oh, they were just doing their jobs. Who decided what jobs those people would hold? They did. They know the nature of their work is to tear down and not to build up. They know that the more dirt they find on people, the better they look and doing their job. They are the life thieves.

The Blessing

Any man is a star to his children, especially if he plans to leave them a good inheritance. When the name, reputation of that man is good, they will have a good inheritance. But if it is defamed the good inheritance withers away. Sometimes it's ripped from that man's hands. He should have had the pleasure of handing it to his children as a blessing, just as Abraham Blessed Isaac.

The blessing sounds nice, doesn't it? It is. I'm talking about the real, tangible, physical property that a father transfers to his children. Being able to give this blessing is a real promise of God. But if you are not in order with God, how can you expect to have the promises? How can you expect to pass the blessing on if you don't *have* the blessing? The Bible says that God gives us **power** to get wealth, so we must need power to get wealth, and our children must need *power* to <u>receive</u> wealth and other blessings.

Until our children get their own spiritual power, they are under ours. Until they reach the age of accountability, their Grace is on the accounts of their parents--, us.

See how you just don't have a responsibility to provide in the natural for your children--, shoes, houses and clothes, but also spiritually. You have the responsibility to provide spiritual covering and grace for them, to protect them until they reach the age of spiritual accountability.

God has promised to rebuke the devour for your sake. He has promised to give His angels charge over you and to keep you in all your ways. He has promised to bless you and make you a blessing. God has promised you so much. Read The Book. But if you're not in line with God, then you are subject to be **among some thieves** at any time. You are at risk of having things taken, even the life you've built for yourself in your future.

We are *among some thieves*--, all kinds. They're peace thieves, time thieves, health thieves, even life thieves out there. Stay with God so He can protect you, your good name, keep your excellent reputation and give you Joy as you travel through life. He will give you the blessing and allow you the power, ability, and Joy of passing The Blessing onto your own children.

CHAPTER EIGHTEEN

AMONG SOME THIEVES

There's a saying that there is honor among thieves, even among thieves. They say that there are certain unspoken rules on the street. There are certain guidelines and an unspoken courtesy or respect that even thieves show one another. I don't believe it.

The respect spoken of in the street life is based on fear and not love. Since it is based on fear, it is not true respect. Respect is how you treat the person who is not in the room. I don't know of any thief or gang stuff for that matter. Who would respect his arch enemy if that enemy didn't have a band of thugs, a collection of weapons and a willingness to use them? That deferential behavior is not because of love, that's fear. So, I'm not talking about that today.

There was a certain man in Jesus this time who took a walk from one city to another. It was about a day's journey. In the course of that travel. He fell *among thieves*. I'll call them, robbers-- pirates. Were they in *wait* for him? Did they know his routine? Did he have valuables? Was this a random act of violence? *A walk by?*

in those days, people walked everywhere; few had horses. Some had donkeys. Fewer had chariots. Today, people talk about the dangers of highways, speed limits, reckless, and drunk drivers, consider that at least you have a car, a metal frame and two to six lockable doors to protect you from passersby. Think about it.

Anyway.

A certain man went down from Jerusalem to Jericho and fell among thieves.

(Luke 10:30, emphasis added).

Over the years, we've usually talked about the Good Samaritan, but today I'm here to talk about the man who fell *among some thieves*. This man was going about his daily business when he fell among some thieves who robbed him and took his clothes. In that day, your clothes said who you were; so they took his identity. They took his identity and left him as though he were no one. But if he were fit to rob, he had status, finances, position and possibly station in life. He was *someone*. But they beat him, and left him for dead.

Why do people rob one another? People are so greedy, lustful and covetous, that they take the property of others to use or sell as their own.

When asked about her stealing, a young woman said that she couldn't help herself. When she sees something that she wants, she says it is so important for her to have it that she figures the person she's taking it from *won't mind* because having it will bring **_her_** so much pleasure. She's not saved.

But many who are saved are so deceitful of heart that they would even rob God. God is so smooth in the way he lets us do things on our honor. The Holy Spirit is ever with us, but He's not standing over us as a task master over a slave. God gives us His trust. We can use it as trust or we can misuse it and cause it to become as a rope to hang ourselves.

Malachi 3, the famous Scripture reads, **Will a man Rob God?** Rob is such a nice word. It's so nice that people use it for man's name. It's short for Robert, but what's a robber but a thief?

The telling of the story doesn't end with a man passing from Jerusalem to Jericho. Through the ages, that story has been sorrowfully told again and again. People have been robbed, burgled, cheated, and stolen from since then.

189

Even I know another man who fell *among thieves*, Jesus was His name. Jesus was hung *among thieves*. He hung on that cross, flanked on either side by men sentenced to die. Who was on either side of Him? Murderers, prostitutes, liars? No, Luke calls them malefactors. What does that mean? Robbers. He hung *among some thieves*.

But before He was on the Cross, He fell into the hands of Judas, his own personal thief, who sold him for 30 pieces of silver. Here's why I called Judas Jesus' own personal thief. Judas joined Jesus and the others, either as a friend or a Disciple. Perhaps Judas saw how much money Jesus and the eleven were taking in and decided that it was the ministry for him. Perhaps he followed after Jesus' popularity being the foremost ministry of the day. Maybe Judas was genuine at first, or maybe not. Maybe he pretended to be friends and brothers with the other 12 for three and a half years, which means he *cased* the Disciples.

Jesus had only a 3 1/2-year ministry, and this character, Judas was there the whole time. Just waiting to take it down. That was a substantial investment of time and energy on Judas' part, to set up a robbery.

Judas epitomized and personified the *Word* thief.. How can you *sell* something that is not even yours? **Judas stole the money and sold Jesus. That means that Judas *trafficked* in humans. Like the Babylonians,** (Revelations 18:13). **Judas was a *soul* seller.**

Robbery was punishable by death in those days and the robbers that hung on either side of Jesus were on their way to hell. Robbers are simply thieves. Jesus, innocent of any crime, was stuck between them. As was the man lying by the side of the road, Jesus was hurt bad, and hanging on a Cross.

Why was Jesus wounded? **For your transgressions.**

Why was Jesus bleeding? **For your healing, by His stripes, you were healed.**

Why was Jesus hurt? For your iniquity. **His bruises are for *our* iniquity.**

Stripped of his clothing and left half dead. The chastisement of our peace was upon Him. **He was crucified for our salvation.**

But he was wounded for our transgressions. He was bruised for our iniquities. The chastisment of our peace was upon him and with his stripes we are healed, (Isaiah 53:6).

Why must we be robbers when all that is asked is our tithes and offerings? Small change. If you could or had to pay for salvation, how much do you think it would cost? $1,000,000? 10 million? Priceless. Who can guess?

What if God required 90% of the income of your entire life? Yet it is so simple. Love the Lord with all your heart, your mind, your soul and your strength. Love your neighbor as yourself. Pay your tithes. 10%. Give generous offerings, cheerfully. If we do not give to God what is due Him, then we rob Him.

There was a man traveling through a wilderness who fell **among thieves**. There was God in flesh called Jesus, who fell *among thieves*, first with Judas, who sold Him out to the Sanhedrin Council (Pharisees & Sadducees). Then he was handed over to the Romans, who had no rights to do what they did to an innocent man. But, like the man in the Parable, they stole His clothes, trying to strip Him of His identity. Then finally, on the cross of Calvary, Jesus was crucified *among some thieves.*

Jesus came to save us from sin and then left us the Holy Spirit. He left us the Comforter in a time when we really need help in our life, our health, our finances, and in our walk with the Lord. And these days, where we really need the *Spirit of Truth*, the

Spirit of Wisdom, we pray that the mind that was in Christ will also be in us. In a day when we pray for the *anointing* in our daily lives, in our ministry and in the lives of our loved ones.

If you had ever fallen **among some thieves**, wouldn't you be careful not to let it happen again? And unnamed man alongside the road between Jerusalem and Jericho fell **among some thieves**. Jesus the Christ on the Cross fell **among some thieves**, and now as we pray and sing the song, Anointing Fall on Me, we are asking for the anointing of God. The anointing which breaks the yokes and destroys bondages which we desperately need in these times. The *anointing* that Jesus came to provide for us, we need it to fall on us. We need it to fall from Heaven. We needed to fall in our situations, to fall on our plans, families, finances, even on our body to heal it. We continue to plead, beg, pray and sing, *Anointing fall on me.*

ANOINTING FALL ON ME

And it shall come to pass in that day that his burden shall be taken away from off my shoulder and his yoke from off thy neck, and the yoke shall be destroyed because of the anointing (Isaiah 10:27).

The anointing (*Christos*) is the power of the Holy Spirit. But the anointing doesn't fall **among thieves** anymore. Jesus did that; He's been there. He's done that, and we know the mind of Jesus is operating with the fullness of Wisdom and He's using His mind, the Mind of Christ at 100%.

He's no dummy, and neither are His Disciples.

Are you giving where you are receiving spiritual lessons? Are you tithing the full amount to your local church? If you don't have a local church, are you tithing where you are being spiritually fed? Or are you robbing God in your tithes and offerings? A tithe is still God's purse. Don't be like Judas who was stealing from the treasury. Don't mistake God's Mercy, Trust, and Love for you as God not knowing; He knows, He's Omniscient.

Judas misused trust to hang himself.

God is so merciful to us; in His great compassion, He allows us in His presence, but it would be better to *not* go into that holiest of places than to go in as a thief or a liar and have to be brought out dead. The same applies to the robbers of the crosses flanking Jesus. They robbed and they reaped death, except the one who asked Jesus to remember him. God wants you to worship Him in Spirit and in truth. He's looking for worshippers.

Thieves are not worshippers.

Come out from **among the thieves**. Come into the holy of Holy's, come into worship.

The tithe is part of Thanksgiving and praise. It is what you give to God for what he has done for you. The offering is your worship and adoration for who He is and shows your faith that He will do for you in the future.

As the Law of Sow & Reap is still working in the Earth, as Seedtime & Harvest remains, it is critical, crucial that you realize that if you are robbing God, not only may the full power of the Holy Spirit be withheld from you, but as you sow, you must reap. If you're robbing someone, especially if it is God, then you've set yourself up to potentially reap robbery and thievery at some time in your life. That is, as you have done it unto the least, you've done it unto him, (Matthew 25:40). If you're robbing anyone then you could be in danger of being robbed, held up. You should fear thieves. If you are one, there's no honor among thieves. Neither is there any spiritual protection for them.

But if you bite and devour one another take heed that you be not consumed

one of another (Galatians 5:15).

195

It's not too late; repent. He is faithful and just to forgive you and cleanse you from all unrighteousness, (1 John 19). Pay your tithes and offerings unto the Lord and come out from **among some thieves**.

Surely we do not expect The Holy Spirit to also fall *among some thieves*.

OUT FROM AMONG SOME THIEVES PRAYER

Dear Heavenly Father, in the Name of Jesus, I thank You the Lamb of God.

Thank You, Lord, that You sent Jesus to fall ***among some thieves*** in my stead. When I did not deserve salvation, when I didn't deserve Mercy and Grace. You provided it for me. Thank You, Lord. Thank You, Father.

Thank You, Lord, for this teaching book that is exposed many categories of thieves that look out there in the world. Search my heart, O Lord, and make me right with You. Lord, I repent of the times that I've robbed You.

I repent of the times that I've have been a thief.

Thank you, Lord, for Jesus, redemptive work at Calvary. I am redeemed from the Curse of the Law (Galatians 3:13), which made me a ***thief***. Thank You, Lord, that I'm no longer a thief, and no longer a robber. Thank You, Lord, for Eternal Life, which is the free gift from You. Thank You for hearing my confession of sin and washing my sin as white as snow.

I thank You, Lord that I am no longer a sinner, and no longer a Thief, that I've come out from ***among thieves***. I thank You for showing me thieves and their tricks. I resolve this day, by the power of the Holy Spirit to serve You in obedience and cheerfulness, and Joy. I am not a robber or thief anymore. And not to be robbed or stolen from again. Thank You, Lord.

I vow to pay my tithes, give my offerings cheerfully and keep wise stewardship over all my increase, in Jesus' Name.

Amen.

Books by this author

AK: Adventures of the Agape Kid

AMONG SOME THIEVES

Ancestral Powers

As My Soul Prospers

Behave

Churchzilla (Wanna-Be Bride of Christ)

The Coco-So-So Correct Show

Demonic Cobwebs

Demonic Time Bombs

Demons Hate Questions

Do Not Orphan Your Seed

Do Not Work for Money

Don't Refuse Me Lord

Every Evil Bird

Evil Touch

The FAT Demons

Fruit of the Womb: Prayers Against Barrenness, *Book 2*

got Money?

Let Me Have a Dollar's Worth

Living for the NOW of God

Lord, Help My Debt

Lose My Location

Made Perfect In Love

The Man Safari *(I'm Just Looking)*

Marriage Ed., *Rules of Engagement & Marriage*

Motherboard: *Key to Soul Prosperity*

My Life As A Slave

Name Your Seed

Plantation Souls

The Poor Attitudes of Money

Power Money: Nine Times the Tithe

The Power of Wealth

Prayers Against Barrenness, For Success in Business and Life, *Book 1*

Seasons of Grief

Seasons of War

Second Marriage, Third Marriage any Marriage

SOULS in Captivity

Soul Prosperity: Your Health & Your Wealth

The *spirit* of Poverty

This Is *NOT* That: How to Keep Demons from Coming at You

The Throne of Grace, *Courtroom Prayers*

Warfare Prayer Against Poverty

When the Devourer is Rebuked

The Wilderness Romance

Other Journals & Devotionals by this author:

The Cool of the Day – Journal

got HEALING? Verses for Life

got HOPE? Verses for Life

got WISDOM? Verses for Life

got GRACE? Verses for Life

got JOY? Verses for Life

got LOVE? Verses for Life

He Hears Us, Prayer Journal

I Have A Star, Dream Journal

I Have A Star, Guided Prayer Journal,

J'ai une Etoile, Journal des Reves

Let Her Dream, Dream Journal *in colors*

Men Shall Dream, Dream Journal,

My Favorite Prayers (in 4 styles)

My Sowing Journal

Tengo una Estrella, Diario de Sueños

Illustrated children's books by Dr. Miles

Big Dog (8-book series)

Do Not Say That to Me

Every Apple

Fluff the Clouds

I Love You All Over the World

Imma Dance

The Jump Rope

Kiss the Sun

The Masked Man

Not During a Pandemic

Push the Wind

Tangled Taffy

What If?

Wiggle, Wiggle; Giggle, Giggle

Worry About Yourself

You Did Not Say Goodbye to Me

www.ingramcontent.com/pod-product-compliance
Lightning Source LLC
LaVergne TN
LVHW052024080426
835513LV00018B/2144